# RIGHT, WRONG AND RACE

Understanding America's Principles

## JERRY MCMULLEN

© Jerry McMullen, PhD

# RIGHT, WRONG AND RACE

World Ahead Press is a division of WND Books. The views and opinions expressed in this book are those of the author and do not necessarily reflect the official policy or position or WND Books.

Paperback ISBN: 978-1-944212-30-8
eBook ISBN: 978-1-944212-31-5

*Printed in the United States of America*
16 17 18 19 20 21 LSI 9 8 7 6 5 4 3 2 1

## THIS BOOK IS DEDICATED TO

My family, whom I love dearly,
and all the courageous people who stand up for what is right.

# CONTENTS

# INTRODUCTION

I began writing this social commentary on February 24, 2014, the day my urologist told me that I had prostate cancer. He shared over the phone that my biopsy revealed cancer with "aggressive features." He provided details during our face-to-face meeting. As we spoke, he slid a copy of the results across the desk so that I could see the findings. I knew Gleason scores were indicators of tumor aggressiveness, with scores between 2 and 6 showing low-grade cancer, a score of 7 suggesting an intermediate grade that will grow at a moderate rate, and scores in the 8 to 10 range revealing high-level aggressiveness. Twelve needle biopsies were removed from my prostate and labeled with letters A through L.

As the doctor spoke, I scanned the sheet and saw nothing but bad news: specimen B, 10; specimen D, 10; specimen E, 10. In total, six of the twelve samples were 10s. The numbers were accompanied by words like adenocarcinoma and high-grade prostatic intraepithelial neoplasia. I looked at the doctor and said, "This looks awful." He candidly reported that my biopsy was among the worst he had ever seen. He paused and modified his statement, explaining, "No, it is the worst."

My neural circuits lit like a Christmas tree. Females and males typically respond differently to stress. Females favor a *tend or befriend* mode, where the biological instinct is to connect with a support network. Natural responses for males are *fight or flight*. I have always been a fighter, so my adrenalin and other fight-related neurohormones surged. The problem was this adversary cannot be taken out with a punch. The battle is more complex and results often appear capricious. Tests have to be run, analyses made, and treatment designed and implemented. All of this takes time. Faith and patience are required. I have abundant faith. Patience is harder for me to come by.

My initial thoughts involved a series of woulda, coulda, shouldas. I should have had regular physicals. I should have had a biopsy earlier and not postponed it, assuming my elevated PSA score was a byproduct of chronic prostatitis. Scenarios of cancer outcomes for friends and family members circulated through my mind. My thoughts raced to the impact my death would have on those I love the most, my wife, kids, and grandkids. I considered my own memorial service and generated variations on that theme. Each morning I woke up feeling queasier. I needed an outlet and I turned to writing.

Following surgery, thirty-four radiation treatments, and hormone therapy, my cancer went into remission. The prognosis was good, my system calmed, and my need for an outlet diminished. My writing pace slowed, but the depth of feelings regarding the topic of this book only grew stronger.

## RATIONALE AND OBJECTIVE

I chose to write this book because I have, for a long time, been concerned about America's future. This is a smoldering issue with me. I fear that our nation is in a downward spiral that will cause hardships for my children and grandchildren. I firmly believe that politicians and the media are ruining our nation. They are not objective. They are not honest. They are cowards. They obfuscate our nation's moral compass. Their sense of right and wrong is driven by a perverse sense of political correctness and fear of criticism rather than social reality. They are afraid of truth, and race is the elephant in the room.

This book has three primary objectives. First, to challenge Bernie Sander's socio-political belief, shared by many, that America was created on "racist principles." Second, to show the hypocrisy of "hands up, don't shoot," "black lives matter," and "white privilege" catchphrases, using the Michael Brown/Darren Wilson and Henry Louis Gates/James Crowley confrontations as case studies. Third, to demonstrate Barack Obama's presidential legacy is one of racial bias and divisiveness.

To accomplish these objectives, Chapter 1 reviews the meaning of principles and their relationship to morality and character. It also provides an overview of the two Protestant groups most responsible for shaping America's character, the Puritans and Scotch-Irish. Chapter 2 offers a practical framework for defining good citizenship and evaluating the impact of specific types of behavior at the personal and social levels. I developed these precepts working as a psychologist in schools for forty years. Although designed for schools, they also translate to broader social contexts. Chapter 3 is a case study of the Michael Brown shooting in Ferguson, Missouri. Ethical and social criteria identified in the first two chapters are used to examine his school, his mindset, his behavior at the time of his death, as well as the event's aftermath. Chapter 4 is dedicated to taking a closer look at Dorian Johnson, Brown's friend who was with him when he robbed a convenience store and engaged in a deadly altercation with police officer Darren Wilson. Special attention is given to the media's handling of Johnson and to his inflammatory comments, such as "shot like an animal" and the influential "Hands up, don't shoot" report that was not supported by the grand jury investigation. Chapter 5 looks at Barack Obama's role and accomplishments as a community organizer in Chicago, and how this experience foreshadowed his presidential approach and legacy. Chapter 6 is a case study that includes Barack Obama's racially-biased/anti-police commentary regarding the incarceration of Harvard professor Henry Louis Gates Jr. by Cambridge police officer Sgt. James Crowley, where Obama declared police "acted stupidly." This chapter considers several associated players in the case, including Harvard University, Charles Ogletree, Deval Patrick, E. Denise Simmons, and Van Jones. Chapter 7 compares and contrasts socio-political ideas of Barack Obama and Jason L. Riley and considers their effectiveness for identifying and solving problems in troubled black communities. An afterword is included to provide a personal narrative that touches on the issues of race relations and personal values.

This book's ultimate intent is to break through the noise that too often dominates discussions about race by providing objective ethical and social criteria for delineating right from wrong, and to clarify effective avenues for achieving personal and social wellbeing. The only way we can move forward rather than regress as a nation is to agree upon common sense principles of good citizenship, then judge every individual according to their actions rather than any demographic variable.

# CHAPTER 1

# AMERICA'S CHARACTER

*Character is shaped, albeit indirectly, by public forces: by general opinion, by neighborhood expectations, by artistic conventions, by elite understandings - in short, by the ethos of the times.*

- JAMES Q. WILSON

Critics of America, decrying the behavior of law enforcement officers, as well as the perceived "victimization" of blacks and "privilege" of whites, have dominated the media following the deadly clash between Michael Brown and Darren Wilson in Ferguson, Missouri. News outlets broadcast unrelenting one-sided messages. These storylines become influential, because if you say it often enough, with enough feeling, it must be true. These critics are wrong and should be challenged. I want to begin my challenge by examining a view expressed by Democratic presidential candidate Bernie Sanders—but shared by others.

An interviewer asked Sanders the following question during a September 14, 2015, speech at Liberty University: "If you were elected president what would you do to bring healing and resolution to the issue of racism in our country?"

Sanders' reply included the following statement: "And I would also say that as a nation, the truth is, that a nation which in many ways was created, and I'm sorry to have to say this, from way back on racist principles, that's a fact . . ." [1] Based on this and other campaign-trail comments, it is clear that Sanders believes America is racist at its core. He offers self-affirmation by assuring anyone who will listen that his opinion is "fact" and "truth."

Bernie Sanders and his like-minded associates will never find solutions to our social problems because they begin with faulty hypotheses. Two things are essential for challenging his opinion. First is understanding the definition and importance of principles. Second is analyzing the principles that shaped America's character, identifying what they are and where they came from.

## ETHICAL PRINCIPLES

Sanders' use of the word "principles" should not be taken lightly. Principles are the foundation of morality and law. They represent the "oughts" of behavior, delineating right from wrong and good from bad. Agreeing upon well-defined principles frees us from what Bernard Williams calls "vulgar relativism." Louis P. Pojman emphasized that ethical/moral principles have at least four related purposes: 1) to keep society from falling apart; 2) to ameliorate human suffering; 3) to promote human flourishing; and, 4) to resolve conflicts of interest in just ways.[2]

Shared principles establish a moral foundation that increases social cohesion, and both individuals and society reap the benefits. Adapting a framework from Pojman, it is evident that principles are not value neutral. We have to judge their impact on behavior, consequences, character, and motives.

| | |
|---|---|
| Behavior or acts | that may be right, wrong, or permissible |
| Consequences | that are good, bad, or indifferent |
| Character | that is virtuous or vicious |
| Motives | that are based on good will or bad will[3] |

Value judgments are essential because consequences matter. Character is right in the middle of this process.

## CHARACTER

There was a time in America, especially during the nineteenth and early twentieth centuries, when character was the focus of both social and political movements. It was clearly defined with virtues such as honesty, thrift, kindness, humility, perseverance, and courage. Character was perceived as the *sine qua non* of child development. Today, such character traits are not defined as clearly or promoted as consistently. There is less accountability. Where excuses are made and virtues compromised, we see an increase in human suffering and failure to flourish.

More than 400 years before Christ, Aristotle's *Nicomachean Ethics* emphasized virtues as a path to happiness and well-being. For him, a person could never be truly happy without good character, which he equated with moral virtue or "excellence." In the East, Buddha (ca. 560 BC) offered the same message—virtues provide the foundation for living a "good" life.[4] Our greatest moral philosophers understood that character matters. Shared principles of right and wrong are essential for social cohesion.

Modern psychological theory supports these philosophical notions. In his book, *Emotional Intelligence: Why It Can Matter More Than IQ*, Daniel Goleman offered the following thoughts in a section titled "Character, Morality, and the Arts of Democracy." He wrote,

> *There is an old-fashioned word for the body of skills that emotional intelligence represents: character. . . . If character development is a foundation of democratic societies, consider some ways emotional intelligence buttresses this foundation. The bedrock of character is self-discipline; the virtuous life, as philosophers since Aristotle have observed, is based on self-control. A related keystone of character is being able to motivate and guide oneself, whether in doing homework, finishing a job, or getting up in the morning. And, as we have seen, the ability to defer gratification and to control and channel one's urges to act is a basic emotional skill, one that in a former day was called will.* [5]

Teddy Roosevelt, more than any other American president, used the bully pulpit to emphasize the importance of character. These are some of his thoughts: [6]

> *"Character is far more important than intellect in making a man a good citizen or successful at his calling—meaning by character not only such qualities as honesty and truthfulness, but courage, perseverance and self-reliance."*

> *"If a man does not have an ideal and try to live up to it, then he becomes a mean, base and sordid creature, no matter how successful."*

In a May, 1900, article in *St. Nicholas* magazine called, "The American Boy," Roosevelt offered the following description of the traits we should instill in our sons (and daughters): "He must not be a coward or a weakling, a bully, a shirk or a prig. He must work hard and play hard. He must be clean-minded and clean-lived, and able to hold his own under all circumstances and against all comers."

How do we develop character? The answer is straightforward. Character is defined by our habits. The following maxim, presented by Scottish author and government reformer Samuel Smiles (1812–1904) in *Life and Labor*, offers a simple but powerful explanation of character formation and its influence on our lives: Sow a thought, and you reap an act; Sow an act, and you reap a habit; Sow a habit, and you reap a character; Sow a character, and you reap a destiny.[7]

This is a variation of Aristotle's observation that, "We are what we repeatedly do. Excellence, then, is not an act, but a habit." Of course, this conceptualization is a double-edged sword. The wrong thoughts, acts, and habits lead to misery rather than excellence.

Martin Luther King Jr. offered the following aspiration in his most famous speech: "I have a dream that my four little children will one day live in a nation where they will not be judged by the color of their skin but by the content of their character." This is a worthy goal. In order to reach this goal, we must understand character, operationally define it, and use it to establish expectations and evaluate individuals. There should be no exceptions or excuses. If we truly believe in the importance of principles and character, we must walk the walk as well as talk the talk.

## AMERICA'S CHARACTER

The United States of America was built on Christian, not racist, principles. To think otherwise is to demonstrate ignorance of our history. During our nation's foundational years, two groups exerted the strongest influence on the principles shaping the unique American character, the Puritans and the Scotch-Irish.

## THE PURITANS

The years 1630–1640 saw the Great Migration of Puritans come from England to America as they fled religious persecution from the Church of England. The Bible was their sole authority, and the spiritual health of their family and community was deemed most important. They accomplished amazing things as they settled in America.[8]

Within five years of founding Massachusetts, they established schools so that all children would be able to read the Bible. The "Old Deluder Act" was passed in 1647. This law began, "It being one chief project of that old deluder, Satan, to keep men from the knowledge of the Scriptures . . . " This law required every township with fifty households to teach all children to read and write. Any town with one hundred families or householders was mandated to "set up a grammar school, the master thereof being able to instruct youth so far as they may be fitted for the university."[9] Towns not adhering to this requirement were required to pay penalties until such schools were in place.

In 1636, the Puritans established Harvard College with the primary intent of training ministers. The earliest rules for Harvard included this statement: "Let every student be plainly instructed and earnestly pressed to consider well the main end of his life and studies is, to know God, and Jesus Christ which is eternal life" (John 17:3). And therefore to lay Christ in the bottom is the only foundation of all sound knowledge and learning."[10] The Puritan belief in strong families, strict morals, education, and hard work yielded prosperity as the byproduct.

## THE SCOTCH-IRISH

Scotch-Irish Protestants immigrated to America from Scotland and Northern Ireland during the eighteenth and nineteenth centuries. It should be noted that "Scotch-Irish" is an Americanism. This group also is referred to as Scot, Scot-Irish, Northern Irish, and Ulster Irish. They preceded the Roman Catholic Irish who came to America en masse during the Potato Famine of 1845–1852.

The first "great migration" of Scotch-Irish occurred between 1717 and 1770. They left their homeland in response to the oppression of parliamentary regulation, low wages, and high rents imposed by absentee landlords. Most Scotch-Irish entered America through Philadelphia then headed westward to settle in the hills of Pennsylvania. They expanded the western frontier, cleared the land, fought the battles, and afforded a buffer of safety for Pennsylvania's pacifist Quakers. Beyond their rugged dispositions and experience as fighters, the Scotch-Irish brought strong moral beliefs and a love of education that was rooted in the Scottish Enlightenment. [11, 12]

## THE SCOTTISH ENLIGHTENMENT

Emphasis on education in Scotland was boosted when the Education Act of 1496 launched a network of parish schools to educate the sons of barons and important freeholders. In 1560, John Knox's *Book of Disciplines* called for a national system of education through the church that would enable every child to read the Bible. The Scottish government passed 1696's School Setting Act, requiring each parish to establish a school that would be free to students.

By 1720, Scotland had the highest literacy rate in Europe at 55 percent. Although much smaller in population, Scotland had five universities compared to only two in England during the seventeenth century. The Royal College of Physicians of Edinburgh, founded in 1681, was the leading center for medicine and science. Clubs such as the Political Economy Club, the Select Society, and the Poker (as in fireplace poker) Club were established in major cities as gathering places where intellectuals exchanged ideas. By the eighteen hundreds, this educational system generated the "democratic myth" that a *lad o' pairts* (a clever or talented individual) could *rise up* through the system to assume high office.[13]

Eighteenth-century Scotland created an unprecedented surge in scientific and intellectual advancement. Among the many notables of this era were the following men: Joseph Black (1728–1799), physicist and chemist who was the first to isolate carbon dioxide; Robert Burns (1759–96), poet; Adam Ferguson (1723–1816), considered the father of sociology; David Hume (1711–1776), philosopher and essayist; James Hutton (1726–1797), founder of modern geology; William Smellie (1740–1795), editor of the first edition of the Encyclopedia Britannica; Adam Smith (1723–1790), philosopher and pioneer of political economics; James Watt (1736–1819), inventor of the first practical steam engine, a key component in launching the Industrial Revolution; and, Thomas Reid (1710–1796), moral philosopher.[14] These men and their Scottish cohorts changed the world in positive and lasting ways. Bruce Lenman observed their "central achievement was a new capacity to recognize and interpret social patterns."[15] Scotch-Irish immigrants transported their ideas, attitudes, and aptitudes to America.

## THOMAS REID

Calvinistic Presbyterian beliefs and values were a driving force during the Scottish Enlightenment. An Enlightenment figure with strong impact on shaping the principles and character of America was philosopher Thomas Reid, founder of the Scottish School of Common Sense Realism.[16, 17, 18] Reid's moral philosophy included three central features: "first principles," "common sense," and "will."[19]

*First Principles.* In *The Intellectual Powers of Man*, Reid stated, "For, before men can reason together, they must agree in first principles; and it is impossible to reason with a man who has no principles in common with you."[20] He elaborated on the nature of these principles in *Essays on the Active Powers of Man*. He stated that conscience is the moral faculty that allows us to discern "the conceptions of right and wrong in human conduct, of merit and demerit, of duty and moral obligation, . . . first principles of morals are the dictates of this faculty . . ."[21]

Reid's first principles include the following commitments: doing our duty as far as we know it, and to fortify our minds against every temptation to deviate from it; preferring a greater good, though more distant, to a less; and a less evil to a greater; understanding that no man is born for himself only; and, believing in and venerating the existence, the perfections, and the providence of God."[22] Those guided by Reid's teaching believed in piety, duty, self-control, modesty, and charity.

*Common Sense.* The general definition of common sense is the ability to perceive, understand, and evaluate things in a way that is common to humanity.

Reid felt that man has an innate, God-given ability to grasp these "first principles" or "self-evident truths." He noted, "Anything that is manifestly contrary to them, is what we call absurd."[23]

Common Sense Realism influenced America's founding fathers, including Thomas Jefferson, John Adams, and John Witherspoon, as they attempted to design a system of government that would effectively address the "common concerns of life." This group stayed remarkably focused while charting the course for America's independence and providing direction for the fledgling nation. It is no coincidence that Thomas Paine's polemical pamphlet was titled *Common Sense*. This work is considered one of the most influential publications of all time, affecting both the American and French Revolutions.

*Will or Free Will.* Reid's theory of "will" hinges on the definitions of "necessity" and "liberty." *Necessity* suggests that a person's behavior is controlled by outside forces or circumstances. This notion was abhorrent to Reid, who wrote: "The lowest of the vulgar have, in all ages, been prone to have recourse to this necessity, to exculpate themselves or their friends in what they do wrong, though, in the general tenor of their conduct, they act upon the contrary principle."[24] Individuals allowing their behavior to be dictated by "necessity" compromise their humanity. They relinquish their greatest gift, the power of reason and choice.

The alternative to "necessity" is "liberty" or "moral liberty." *Moral liberty* involves acting in accordance with a standard that is independent from external forces. In Reid's view, God grants us liberty so that we can make moral decisions by using our *will power*. Virtues establish a "fixed purpose or resolution" to act. Our character is defined by our virtues, our will, and our actions. Virtues are validated through common sense. Will power provides moral muscle to make choices. Reid said, "Moral Liberty does not merely consist of the power of doing what we will, but in the power of willing what we will."[25] Without moral reason, we are ruled by passions, such as base desires and appetites.

## JOHN WITHERSPOON.

John Witherspoon (1723–1794) was a major catalyst for disseminating Common Sense Realism throughout America. He was born in Gifford, Scotland, earning a Master of Arts degree from the University of Edinburgh and a Doctorate in Divinity from Saint Andrew's University. He served as a Presbyterian minister from 1758-1768, writing works on theology that bolstered his reputation as a scholar and activist. At the strong and persistent urging of noted American physician and patriot Benjamin Rush, who studied medicine at Edinburgh University, Witherspoon and his family came to America in 1768 so that he could become president of the College of New Jersey, which became Princeton University. As president, he was responsible for teaching courses in moral philosophy, divinity, rhetoric, history and chronology, and French. The school's early emphasis was training men for the ministry.[26]

Witherspoon served as university president from 1768–1795, putting the school on sound academic footing as well as guiding it through the Revolutionary War. In addition to his college presidency, Witherspoon was a signer of the Declaration of Independence. At the Continental Congress meeting where the Declaration was signed, another member argued that the country was "not yet ripe for such a declaration." Witherspoon responded that it "was not only ripe for the measure, but in danger of rotting for the want of it."[27] He served as a New Jersey delegate to the Continental Congress from 1776–1782 and completed two terms in the New Jersey State Legislature.

In his sermons and lectures, Witherspoon demonstrated the influence of Thomas Reid. In *A Princeton Companion* (1978), Alexander Leitch made the following observations about Witherspoon: "He believed . . . morality was a science. It could be cultivated in his students or deduced through the development of the moral sense—an ethical compass instilled by God in all human beings and developed through education (Reid) or sociability (Hutcheson). . . . Witherspoon, in accordance with the Scottish moral sense philosophy, taught that all human beings—religious or otherwise—could be virtuous." Leitch went on to say, "He saw no conflict between faith and reason: instead, he encouraged his students to test their faith by the rule of experience. He was much inclined to apply the test of common sense to any proposition, and to reduce it to its simplest terms."[28]

Witherspoon's wry humor was evident when the New Jersey legislature rejected his proposal to meet before rather than after dinner so that he would be less likely to fall asleep. When the motion failed, he informed his colleagues, "There are two kinds of speaking that are very interesting . . . perfect sense and perfect nonsense. When there is speaking in either of these ways I shall engage to be all attention. But when there is speaking, as there often is, halfway between sense and nonsense, you must bear with me if I fall asleep."[29]

Witherspoon's students went on to do great things. His pupils included President James Madison, Vice President Aaron Burr, thirty-seven judges, three of whom became justices of the US Supreme Court, ten cabinet officers, twelve members of the Continental Congress, twenty-eight US senators, and forty-nine US congressman. Additionally, the university trained Presbyterian ministers who were sent to educate children on America's western frontier.

## WILLIAM HOLMES MCGUFFEY

In many ways, the story of the McGuffeys is typical of the Scotch-Irish. His grandparents, William "Scotch Billy" and Ann (McKittrick) McGuffey, were born in Scotland. They immigrated to America in August 1774 with their three children, including William Holmes McGuffey's father, seven-year-old Alexander. The family landed in Philadelphia then moved to a Scotch-Irish settlement in York County, Pennsylvania, where they purchased a small farm. On May 27, 1779, Scotch Billy joined the Continental Army to fight in the War of Independence. During his service, the family continued farming and opened a small tavern (George Washington drank there.) where Alexander learned about the war by listening to the conversations of patrons. In 1889, the family moved west to Washington County, Pennsylvania, south of Pittsburgh.

At that time, Washington County was still frontier and vulnerable to attacks from a confederation of Indian tribes that included the Shawnee, Miami, Seneca, Delaware, and others. It was common for young Scotch-Irish men to join military operations on the frontier. True to form, Alexander and his friend, Duncan McArthur, who later became governor of Ohio, joined the Pennsylvania volunteers. Alexander served as a scout for General Anthony Wayne during the 1790s.

Alexander married Anna Holmes in 1797, and William Holmes McGuffey was born on September 23, 1800. The family moved to a Mahoning County farm in the Ohio Western Reserve in 1802. Brick and tinplate industries flourished in the region and nearby Youngstown became a major center for America's steel industry. Quintin Skrabec commented about the culture of the region:

> *"The Western Reserve crucible was a mixing bowl of three conservative traditions—New England Puritans, Scotch-Irish, and German. These traditions found common ground in the virtues of thrift, Christian morals, industry, honesty, and perseverance. Covenanter Scotch-Irish and New England Puritans could find much in common. The mixing of the cultures created a hatred of slavery, drunkenness, and war, and a love of education."[30]*

Harvey Minnich also described the personality forged by the merging of these groups: "Here the Puritan ideas were greatly modified or entirely substituted. This new mind—practical German, thrifty Scotch, witty Irish—became cosmopolitan."[31] Beliefs of this cultural alliance led to the formation of the Whig and Republican political parties in the Western Reserve.

William McGuffey's education began with his mother guiding him through Bible readings and memorizations. His first formal schooling came from the

Presbyterian minister William Wick. McGuffey and his sister Jane attended Wick's school in Youngstown, living with the family during the week and returning home on weekends. Reverend Wick reportedly gave William a certificate and suggested that he was ready to become a roving teacher when he was fourteen years old. So, at age fourteen, McGuffey conducted a four-month session of school to tutor the children of twenty-three families in an area that is now Calcutta, Ohio. Forty-eight students attended his subscription school.

McGuffey continued his education with Reverend Thomas Hughes (1769–1828) at Greersburg Academy (a school briefly attended by abolitionist John Brown) in what is now Darlington, Pennsylvania. Hughes was a 1797 graduate of Princeton, suggesting he was a student of John Witherspoon. Following Greersburg, McGuffey enrolled at Washington College where the Reverend Andrew Wylie (1789–1851) became his close friend and mentor. McGuffey emerged as a product of the Scotch-Irish Presbyterians' strong educational mission as they moved westward.

*Cincinnati College of Teachers.* The most important phase of McGuffey's career began when he accepted the 1825 invitation of Reverend Robert Hamilton Bishop to teach at Miami University in Oxford, Ohio, which is thirty-three miles north of Cincinnati. At that time, Cincinnati was at the intellectual forefront of the Western Enlightenment. Just as the Scottish Enlightenment had clubs dedicated to intellectual exchange, Cincinnati had the "College of Teachers." This group included notables such as Albert Pickett (a pupil of Noah Webster), physician Daniel Drake, and Lyman Beecher and Calvin Stow who were professors at Lane Theological Seminary. McGuffey became a key member who profited from the stimulation and support of his colleagues. The College of Teachers was concerned with establishing common schools, providing textbooks suited for "western children," and training professional teachers. Additionally, members such as the Beechers were dedicated social reformers, especially on the topic of slavery. Quentin Skrabec offered this observation of the group's impact:

> *"In the long run, it was not the abolitionist movement of the 1830s that ended slavery, but the moral education of decades that changed attitudes towards slavery. In many ways the 'College of Teachers' offered a model for long-term change. For the 'College of Teachers,' the idea was simple; if you wanted moral behavior in society, then you needed moral education. The impact is not immediate but the result is decisive."[32]*

Skrabec's opinion is supported by the fact that Harriet Elisabeth Beecher Stowe (1811-1896), Lyman Beecher's daughter, energized the abolitionist movement with her publication of *Uncle Tom's Cabin* in 1852. At an 1862 meeting, President Abraham Lincoln reportedly greeted her by saying, "So you are the little woman who wrote the book that started this Great War."

*McGuffey's Eclectic Readers.* Noah Webster (1758–1843) made significant contributions to writing textbooks for American children. His three-volume *Grammatical Institute of the English Language* consisted of a speller (1783), a grammar (1784), and a reader (1785). In addition to teaching children how to read, spell, and pronounce words, the *Blue-Backed Speller* contained a series of moral fables and lengthy moral catechism, which were entirely secular with no mention of God. Skrabec explained: "The catechism used questions and answers to define the moral virtues of humility, industry, mercy, purity of heart, justice, generosity, gratitude, truth, charity, economy, and cheerfulness, and problem emotions and evils such as anger, revenge, and avarice."[33] The *Blue-Backed Speller* became the most popular text of its time, selling fifteen million copies by 1837.

The *Grammatical Institute* also infused principles of patriotism. In Webster's words, "In the choice of pieces, I have not been inattentive to the political interests of America. Several of those masterly addresses of Congress, written at the commencement of the late Revolution, contain such noble, just, and independent sentiments of liberty and patriotism, that I cannot help wishing to transfuse them into the breasts of the rising generation."[34] Among the *Institutes'* politically-oriented content were Thomas Day's essay calling for the abolition of slavery in accordance with the Declaration of Independence and excerpts from Thomas Paine's *The American Crisis*, a series of sixteen pamphlets originally published in the *Pennsylvania Journal*, the first one being signed with the pseudonym of—what else—"Common Sense."

Truman and Smith was a small Cincinnati-based publishing company that wanted to create textbooks adapted for Western schools. The firm invited Catherine Beecher (1800-1878), daughter of Lyman Beecher and sister of Harriet Beecher Stowe, to write the texts. Because her primary interest was higher education for women rather than teaching at the elementary level, she declined their invitation and recommended William McGuffey.

McGuffey had taught elementary grades. When assembling material for his books, he started by gathering neighborhood children to test the appeal of simple poems and stories. His goal was to exploit pioneer children's connection with nature. The *Readers'* content consisted of stories about forests, flowers, animals, and interpersonal relationships. All of this was watched over by a strict but benevolent God. Among the verses and phrases popularized by *McGuffey's Readers* were: "Mary had a little lamb;" "Twinkle, twinkle little star;" "If at first you don't succeed, try, try again;" "Now I lay me down to sleep;" "Crying over spilled milk;" "Tit for tat;" "The Real McCoy;" "Where there's a will, there's a way;" "Waste not, want not;" and, "A friend in need is a friend indeed."

The *First Reader* and *Second Reader* were published in 1836. The *Primer*, *Third Reader*, and *Fourth Reader* followed in 1837. The series was a tremendous success, selling half a million copies by 1843, more than seven million by 1850, and over 122 million by the 1920s. *McGuffey Readers* became the primary text in thirty-seven states. Abraham Lincoln called William McGuffey "Schoolmaster to the Nation." *The Saturday Evening Post* (1941) celebrated McGuffey's impact by noting, "For seventy-five years, his system and his books guided the minds of four-fifths of the school children of the nation in their taste for literature, in their morality, and in their school development, and, next to the Bible, in their religion."[35]

Major industrialists based in Pittsburgh and the Western Reserve, such as Andrew Carnegie, George Westinghouse, Henry Clay Frick (the father of American capitalism), H. J. Heinz, and Andrew Mellon, attained their education through *McGuffey's Readers*. David McCullough described this group as an "early-rising, healthy, hard-working, no-nonsense lot, Scotch-Irish most of them, Freemasons, tough, canny, and without question, extremely fortunate to have been in Pittsburgh at that particular moment in history."[36] No industrialist revered McGuffey more than Henry Ford. In the, *The Young Henry Ford*, biographer Sidney Olson described McGuffey's influence on Ford:

> *"To the end of his days, Ford, like all of his generation, lived in McGuffeyland. It was a wonderful land, with never a juvenile delinquent in it, because old William McGuffey's shrewdly chosen dramatic readings plunged their morals home like hot pokers, scarring the pupils all their lives with a stiff conscience, a clear knowledge of right and wrong, and an ineradicable appetite for Fourth of July oratory."[36]*

John Westerhoff described the principles behind McGuffey's selection of material for his *Readers*: a) We live in an orderly, cause-and-effect world where we reap what we sow and get what we deserve. b) The natural world is beautiful and aspects of nature represent "proud monuments of God." c) Hard work and frugality bring prosperity. The responsibility for success or failure lies with the individual. And, d) those who prosper should be kind and use their wealth in socially responsible ways. Love of country was considered a religious act because America is a gift from God. [38]

The *Readers* were revised five times. Henry H. Vail worked with McGuffey and served as editor for the 1857 and 1879 revisions. By 1879, McGuffey was not directly involved. Vail adapted the *Readers'* content to address the needs of the post-Civil War nation[39]

The mission of the 1879 revision was challenging because the young country had changed so dramatically after the original publication. The Civil War was over, the country needed healing, and the Industrial Revolution was in full swing. The 1879 *Readers'* content aimed to connect with and unite people from very diverse backgrounds and experiences, all struggling to adapt to circumstances that often were brutally harsh. Minnich commented the *Readers* "...fitted the real needs of social, religious, and economic variants fusing into a workable civic unity."[40] Their first principles remained steadfast. They were intended to instill in children a sense of allegiance to their new country, a shared moral sense, and a belief in the right to rise.

Minnich noted the *Readers'* content allowed students to enter "into experiences of the noblest of mankind, statesmen, poets, patriots, philanthropists, teachers, moralists, prophets, spiritual leaders. . . . Each day the dawn of a widening world opened word by word, poem by poem, oration by oration, essay by essay, until the whole realm of earth's worthy spirits became companion to his thoughts."[41] Author Hannibal Hamlin Garland (1860–1940), in *A Son of the Middle Border,* offered the following tribute to the impact of *McGuffey's Readers*:

> *"With a high ideal of the way in which these grand selections should be read, I was scared almost voiceless when it came my turn to read them before the class. "STRIKE FOR YOUR ALTARS AND YOUR FIRES. STRIKE FOR THE GREEN GRAVES OF YOUR SIRES—GOD AND YOUR NATIVE LANDS," always reduced me to a trembling breathlessness. The sight of the emphatic print was a call to the best that was in me and yet I could not meet the test. Excess of desire to do it just right often brought a ludicrous grasp and I often fell back into my seat in disgrace, the titter of the girls adding to my pain. . . .. No matter, we were taught to feel the force of these poems and to reverence the genius that produced them and that was worth while." [42]*

Unfortunately, the breadth, scope, force, clarity, and moral vision of *McGuffey's Readers* is lost in today's textbooks. As a result, students' worldview is narrowed and passion for learning is never ignited for many. They are cheated of a meaningful sense of history, literature, critical thinking, rhetoric, and moral principles. Those looking for evidence of the *Reader's* effectiveness should note the quality of letters presented in the Ken Burns Civil War series. Many of these individuals had no more than elementary school educations utilizing these texts.

## CONCLUSION

America was founded on Christian, not racist principles. Slavery did not begin or end in America. Slavery is mentioned in the *Code of Hammurabi* (ca. 1760 BC). The Qin dynasty in China (221–206 BC) castrated men and made them eunuch slaves. It was a slave class that built the Angkor Wat monuments in Cambodia during the Khmer Empire. Jews were enslaved in Egypt. Islamic invaders enslaved hundreds of thousands of Indians during eighth century invasions. Christians were taken as slaves during the Ottoman wars. In the *Encyclopedia of Human Rights*, Volume 1 (2009), David P. Forsythe stated: "at the beginning of the nineteenth century an estimated three-quarters of all people alive were trapped in bondage against their will either in some form of slavery or serfdom." The continent of Africa has a long history of slavery and it continues to be a problematic area for contemporary slavery.

Slaves came to America when the original colonies were part of the British Empire. In that era, with mankind's long history of slavery in all corners of the world, it is incredible that America could abolish slavery so quickly after winning independence and establishing itself as a nation. Consider the following chronology:

### April 19, 1775

Minutemen and redcoats clash at Lexington and Concord, firing "The shot heard round the world" to begin the American Revolutionary War.

### July 4, 1776

Congress adopts the Declaration of Independence.

### September 3, 1783

Treaty of Paris ends the American Revolutionary War.

### June 21, 1788

United States Constitution is ratified.

### April 30, 1789

George Washington inaugurated as first President of the United States

### April 12, 1861

Civil War begins when Confederate forces fire on Fort Sumter.

## January 1, 1863

Abraham Lincoln issues the Emancipation Proclamation.

## April 9, 1865

Robert E. Lee surrenders at the Appomattox Court House, effectively ending the Civil War.

Before George Washington assumed the presidency in 1789, strong abolitionist sentiments were already in place. Protestant leaders worked passionately to end slavery. The moral principles of abolitionist sentiment escalated into a bloody war. Three hundred and sixty thousand Union soldiers died and another 275,000 were wounded while fighting this conflict. No other nation in history has made such a sacrifice for such a cause.

Ignoring history, Bernie Sanders, Barack Obama, and company continue to promote notions of racism. Ben Shapiro, then editor-at-large for Breitbart News Network, called Sanders' responses during a March 2016 Democratic presidential debate an attempt to "double down on President Obama's strategy of racial polarization for political gain." Sanders' response to the moderator's question regarding his "racial blind spot" included the following statement:

> *When you're white, you don't know what it's like to be living in a ghetto. You don't know what it's like to be poor. You don't know what it's like to be hassled when you walk down the street or you get dragged out of a car. And I believe that as a nation in the year 2016, we must be firm in making it clear. We will end institutional racism and reform a broken criminal justice system.*[43]

Sanders not only tells the harmful socio-political lie that America was founded on racist principles, but he promotes the bigoted notion of "white privilege." How absurd to claim that white people don't know what it's like to be poor or what it's like to be hassled while walking down the street. It's time to challenge these falsehoods.

# CHAPTER 2

# GOOD CITIZENSHIP

*In all the world and in all of life there is nothing more important to determine than what is right.*

- C. I. LEWIS

Principles embraced by the Puritans and Scotch-Irish are by no means exclusive to Protestantism or to America. The morality of all successful civilizations reflects similar values. As Pojman said, such principles are essential to keep society from falling apart, ameliorate human suffering, promote human flourishing, and resolve conflicts of interest in just ways.

While Chapter 1 focused on America's ethical-moral principles and character, this chapter offers a behavioral-social perspective. Michael Brown's death generated an emotional and sometimes violent reaction. Reflecting on the looting and destruction in Ferguson, Missouri, former basketball star Charles Barkley commented, "One of the problems with this entire situation is there's so much noise going on, you never get to the crux of the issue that you need to be discussing."[1] This chapter provides a framework for getting "to the crux of the issue." We need unifying social guidelines that differentiate right from wrong. We need objectivity, understanding, and insights that identify problems and point to solutions.

The following concepts and frameworks were formulated during my forty years working as a school psychologist with a specialty in behavior management. These ideas were developed in but are not limited to schools. Because schools are microcosms of their broader social contexts, the concepts also apply to more extended communities.

## SURVEY REGARDING STUDENT BEHAVIOR

The primary objective of schools should be imparting knowledge and values that enable students to become responsible, productive citizens. The need, as clearly identified by educators such as Noah Webster and William McGuffey, is to develop a shared vision, a common moral base, and patriotism. These men aimed to meld the many into one—Americans with well-delineated beliefs and character. Our original national motto was *E Pluribus Unum*, which means "from many, one." Today, there are many competing voices and a tendency toward "vulgar relativism" regarding ethics and morals.

To explore trends in schools, I opened my training sessions by asking, "Has student behavior changed during the past ten years?" Invariably, the answer was a resounding, "Yes!" Regardless of setting or grade level, the consistency of educator (teachers, administrators, paraprofessionals, and others) response was remarkable. After years of not formally documenting audience responses, I decided to quantify the input. The top ten changes in student behavior listed below are in rank order of their frequency. Responses from urban settings, although similar, differ enough to warrant separate presentation. The suburban and rural sample is based on seventy-five workshops attended by approximately three thousand educators. The urban sample represents nineteen workshops attended by more than one thousand educators.

## EDUCATOR-REPORTED CHANGES IN STUDENT BEHAVIOR

| SUBURBAN AND RURAL | URBAN |
|---|---|
| 1. Less respectful | 1. Less parental involvement and supervision |
| 2. Less parental involvement and supervision | 2. Noncompliant, oppositional, defiant |
| 3. Assume less personal responsibility | 3. Negative attitude, unmotivated |
| 4. Negative attitude, unmotivated | 4. Less respectful |
| 5. Impatient, impulsive, want instant gratification | 5. More aggressive |
| 6. More hurried, stressed, overburdened | 6. More emotional problems (especially anger and hostility) |
| 7. More aggressive | 7. Impatient, impulsive, want instant gratification |
| 8. Too much screen/electronics time | 8. Short attention span |
| 9. Noncompliant, oppositional, defiant | 9. Low self-esteem |
| 10. Home challenges school's authority or veracity (student is right; school is wrong) | 10. Assume less personal responsibility |

Seven of ten changes in student behavior appear on both suburban/rural and urban educators' lists. For discussion purposes, these changes are grouped into three categories: 1) respect and responsibility; 2) motivation, self-control, and compliance; and, 3) parental involvement and supervision.

Across settings, educators reported less respect and personal responsibility. Both samples indicated a trend for students to show disrespect for authority, peers, property, and self. Some students were described as having "no desire for respect." A decline in personal responsibility was linked to students who deny personal accountability, blame others, or use diagnosed medical conditions (e.g., attention-deficit/hyperactivity disorder) to excuse inappropriate behavior. Educators indicated that too many students are not worried about right and wrong. According to one high school teacher, "the gray area has become huge." Some students display a "Teflon mentality," believing that "nothing sticks to me." Demand for character education programs reflects the magnitude of concern regarding declines in respect and responsibility.

Concerns in the areas of motivation, self-control, and compliance are signs of educators' perceptions that too many students exhibit resistance to school personnel and disregard for academics. Jobs, peers, electronics, and social media take priority over schoolwork for some students. Lack of self-control was described as impatience, impulsivity, and inability to delay gratification. In addition, students from preschool through high school were viewed as more aggressive. The learning environment is damaged by students who are brazen, chronically defiant, or violent. They often show no fear of consequences. Chronic noncompliance, opposition, and defiance cause frustration and feelings of futility, driving talented teachers from schools.

Reduced parental involvement and supervision ranked high in frequency for both samples. It is interesting that parenting emerged so pervasively, because it is not a "student behavior." Educators believed that changes in family life impact the way students behave in school. Increased numbers of single-parent and dual-income homes result in less time for parents to help with academics and teach social skills. In addition, parents who are stressed or overwhelmed are more prone to impatience and emotional volatility.

Educators in suburban/rural and urban schools reported many similar changes in student behavior; but, as one might expect, there also are differences. In suburban settings, three salient issues were: 1) hurry, stress, and burden in students' lives; 2) screen time and electronics; and 3) parents who challenge school's authority. For many students, childhood has become an accelerated process. They are saddled with developmentally inappropriate responsibilities (latch-key children, siblings raising siblings). Educators worry because of decreased family stability and family schedules that are overburdened with sports or other activities. Screen/electronic time is perceived as a negative influence because objectionable content such as violence, sex, and inappropriate language is mimicked during interactions with peers and adults. In addition, screen time is a passive, sedentary activity that detracts from homework, physical exercise, and face-to-face peer interaction. Finally, too many suburban parents approach educators with the attitude that their child is right, and the school is wrong.

Responses from urban educators yielded three changes related to emotional issues and attention that do not appear on the list of their suburban counterparts. Increased numbers of urban students are viewed as having emotional and mental health problems that often are expressed through anger or hostility. In addition, higher percentages of students are perceived as having low self-esteem. Short attention spans among urban students are described as inability to focus, stay on task, or follow directions—deficits that pose barriers to learning. The frequency and intensity of problem behavior in urban schools are not necessarily obvious when comparing lists. These differences, which may be amplified by emotion and compounded by stressors in homes and neighborhoods, create greater obstacles for urban educators to overcome.

## WHAT DO THE RESULTS REALLY TELL US?

After years of sharing these "changes in student behavior" during training sessions, I belatedly asked myself, "Do I believe these results?" The answer was "yes" and "no." Walking through schools, many were as fine as any that I've seen. The overwhelming majority of students were well behaved, cooperative, and productive. The worst settings were meat grinders that eroded the physical and emotional well-being of staff and responsible students alike. Overall, I felt there were too many exceptions to the reported trends to qualify them as representing across-the-board changes.

On the other hand, I have great respect for the opinions of those working on the front lines of education. I finally came to the conclusion that audiences were providing the honest answer to a question that was somewhat different from the one posed. They were not identifying *changes* over a ten-year interval. In reality, these astute educators outlined the *most critical obstacles* they face in running effective classrooms and schools. They effectively defined the essential characteristics for productive citizenship as: respect and responsibility; motivation, self-control, and compliance; and, parental involvement and supervision. This makes perfect sense. Behavior running counter to these essentials captures their attention because it compromises classroom instruction and undermines the school's social climate.

These essentials of good citizenship also apply to social contexts beyond schools. Respect, responsibility, self-control, compliance, and strong families produce communities that work together and prosper. I live in such a community, so I know the benefits. On my block, we have multiple races and ethnicities with a shared belief in respect and responsibility. Communities in turmoil, where thriving is secondary to surviving, are characterized by disrespect, irresponsibility, violence, and dysfunctional families. I lived in one of those neighborhoods as well, so I know the hardship imposed by such an environment.

## THE PROSOCIAL HIERARCHY

The *Prosocial Hierarchy* is a framework that I developed to illustrate types of behavior and their related effects. It presents six behavior categories and their respective consequences for individuals (personal outcomes) and the community (social outcomes). These components are organized into three levels: prosocial, negotiation, and antisocial.

## PROSOCIAL HIERARCHY

| LEVEL | BEHAVIOR | Personal Outcome | Social Outcome |
|---|---|---|---|
| PROSOCIAL | MORAL CONDUCT | Character | Cohesion |
| | INITIATIVE | Achievement | Progress |
| NEGOTIATION | COOPERATION | Belonging | Teamwork |
| | OPPOSITION | Stress | Tension |
| ANTISOCIAL | DEFIANCE | Hostility | Conflict |
| | VIOLENCE | Danger | Chaos |

*Prosocial*, at the top of the hierarchy, is the most desirable level of behavior, benefitting both the individual and the community. Initiative fuels achievement and moral conduct establishes a positive and unifying direction.

*Negotiation* is represented by the behaviors of cooperation and opposition. Neither of these is inherently good or bad. Although the former has a positive connotation, history teaches us that cooperation is not always desirable. There are times when we should offer opposition. It is important for individuals and groups to learn how to oppose appropriately and effectively.

*Antisocial* is the descriptor I selected for the bottom of the hierarchy to emphasize that neither individuals nor groups flourish in settings characterized by defiance or violence. It destroys lives and tears the social fabric. These behaviors inevitably erode personal and social well-being.

The *Prosocial Hierarchy* provides an objective tool that can be applied when evaluating the behavior of individuals and groups. The fact is, we reap what we sow. *Behavior matters* because it defines a person's character and destiny, and it impacts outcomes. If we truly want to understand the quality of life in a community or social group, including individual families, we must examine the group's behavior. Results are predictable.

## THE SOCIAL RIPPLE EFFECT

Behavior does not occur in a vacuum. Social systems are marked by reciprocity. The action of each individual impacts the group. How many antisocial individuals does it take to impair a community? My experience in schools led me to develop the informal gauge of social influence called the "Social Ripple Effect" that is illustrated below. The diagram below depicts three groups who exert influence on each other—responsible individuals, knuckleheads, and antisocial disrupters. The arrows represent the force exerted by the groups on one another.

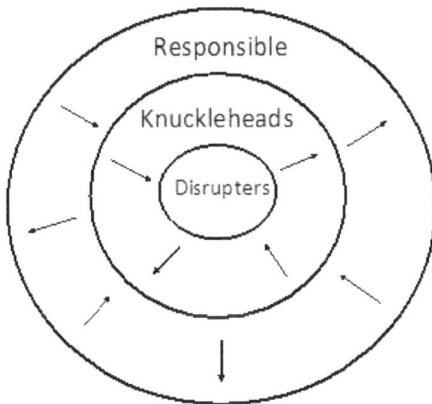

Social Ripple Effect

Responsible
Knuckleheads
Disrupters

Jerry McMullen, Ph.D.

The large outer circle represents responsible individuals, who comprise the majority in any school or community. Traditionally, this group exercised the greatest influence because of status gained through achievements and leadership roles. A middle-school teacher told me that she believes the impact of this group is shrinking because their approach is now characterized by what she called "The Three M's." By this, she meant the responsible group has become increasingly *Meek, Mild, and Mute.* They mind their own business, avoid trouble, and keep opinions to themselves. In essence, they are society's silent majority.

The middle circle depicts knuckleheads. These students are followers who shift behavior in response to dominant role models and peer pressure. If responsible behavior is the norm, they conform; however, if disrupters prevail, they tend to follow their negative example. Knuckleheads compound behavior problems in classrooms and communities when they support and mimic disrupters.

The small inner circle represents antisocial disrupters who are oppositional, defiant, and/or violent. They read hostile intent into the behavior of others, fail to assume responsibility for their actions, and show little remorse or fear of consequences. As their numbers increase, they divert time, resources, and emotional energy away from learning and progress, and toward discipline and crisis intervention. In schools, the magnitude of their defiant/violent disruption distinguishes them from impulsive students who interrupt, hyperactive students who have difficulty remaining seated and controlling physical activity, distractible students who need structure and guidance, unmotivated students who resist school work, and class clowns.

The percentage of antisocial disrupters is a crucial variable for determining a school's behavior management needs. In my experience, it is relatively easy to handle discipline if less than one percent (<1 per 100) of a student population is severely disruptive. *Many* schools I have worked with fall into this category. Schools are stressed when the number of antisocial disrupters reaches five percent, the educational program is seriously damaged at 10 percent and educator bailout-or-burnout occurs at 15 percent.

The negative effect of antisocial disrupters is disproportionate to their numbers. This may explain why none of the top ten behavior changes reported by educators is positive. These behaviors have a destructive impact. To reduce the social influence of severe disrupters, the constructive behavior of responsible students should be validated and reinforced. They should be empowered to express and exert their influence. At the same time, behavior management programs should promote strategies that teach replacement behavior to severe disrupters. For this recalcitrant group, dedicated (and expensive) resources such as behavior management specialists and special education classes are necessary.

Three anecdotes illustrate responsible individuals exerting influence. Part of my approach to behavior management, the *Prosocial Behavior System,* involves a "stop and think" component that was designed by professors at the University of South Florida.[2] Their system includes a five-step sequence for teaching social skills: 1) stop and think; 2) decide if you want to make a good choice or a bad choice; 3) think of the steps needed for the social skill or alternatives to the action; 4) just do it; and, 5) ask "How did I do?" When this program is instituted, "stop and think" and "good choice or bad choice" become part of the language for staff and students.

The first anecdote involved a (white) boy who was classified as a student with social and emotional disturbance. He was reassigned from his home school to a special education facility because of volatile tantrums laced with profanity. His mother, in search of the perfect diagnosis, took him to a developmental neurologist who claimed the boy was on the autism spectrum and explained that his profane verbal outbursts were "complex verbal tics."

During one outburst, the school psychologist, who knew this boy well, escorted him from the classroom into the hallway and tried redirecting him with humor by saying, "Your ears are so red that if we went into a closet and turned out the lights, I think that I could read a book by the light of your ears."

The boy felt a complex verbal tic rise to the surface. He turned to the psychologist and said, "These are not ears. They are sh*t sensors, and they are focused on you." What an amazing tic! As part of the overall assessment, his mother demanded that I evaluate her son. Among other findings, I discovered that his IQ was 142—way high. *This* explained why his verbal tics were so complex.

The same boy was in the hallway throwing another tantrum about two weeks after the "ear" episode. A life skills class (comprised of students with intellectual disabilities, most with measured IQs below 60—very low) was walking down the hall. As the group passed, he glared and yelled "f*ck you" at each student. Finally, a boy with Down syndrome stopped, pointed at him, and said, "He's making a bad choice." This is the Social Ripple Effect in action. You don't have to be combative, but it is useful for peers to label bad choices for what they are.

As it turned out, my diagnostic impression and the perception of the school's staff were correct in considering this boy to be oppositional-defiant rather than autistic. With the help of an outstanding teacher who was well versed in developing prosocial skills, he eventually returned to his home school and excelled in their program for gifted students.

Another example comes from a high school that initiated a school climate committee comprised of staff and students to deal with some volatile issues. Part of their training involved discussing the social ripple effect and the tendency of responsible students to be meek, mild, and mute. One student member of this committee was a petite, feisty sophomore girl who was president of her class. She took the "3M's" message to heart. One day in the cafeteria she (a white girl) and her girlfriends were eating when a student from a nearby table of boys (all black) threw a hamburger patty that hit her girlfriend. To the chagrin of her friends, this young lady picked up the patty, walked to the boys' table and said, "I don't know who threw this, but one of you owes my friend an apology." Immediately, one of the boys jumped to his feet and started shouting about her disrespecting him. She repeated that she didn't know who threw the patty, but said that someone from their table owed an apology. Later in the day, that boy extended an apology.

The final anecdote involves a rural school district that solicited students, educators, *and* community members to define prosocial expectations that would extend beyond schools and into the community. This was a good school district in a solid community with no major problems, but the school district superintendent hoped to make a good thing better. No setting is without some rough edges. He pulled together a large committee. During evening workshops, I provided the group with an overview of prosocial concepts, then asked them to establish expectations for "ways we want our community to be."

When describing the Social Ripple Effect to them, I cited an example from their community. I arrived well before my first presentation so that I could walk around town. I stopped at a popular park that included ramps for skateboarders. The skateboarders were generally well-behaved; they waited their turns, showed off their skills, and enjoyed themselves. One (white) boy was loud and profane. His voice could be heard throughout the park and most sentences included at least one f-bomb. He stood out as different from the others. His rudeness, volume, and profanity dominated the scene. Adults and small children were within earshot. No one said anything to this boy and his behavior went unchallenged. When I shared this observation, the committee took it to heart. The image of a single disruptor going unchallenged made them uncomfortable.

Through several meetings dedicated to finalizing principles for ways they wanted their community to be, courage was a virtue that was always rose to the top. The unchallenged incivility at their park continued to stick in their craw. In their final version, the committee selected Respect, Responsibility, Courage, and Kindness as their *Core Expectations*. These expectations applied not only to students, but also to staff and members of the community. They designed posters that stated -

## MEMBERS OF THE SCHOOL DISTRICT ARE EXPECTED TO:

Act responsibly and take Responsibility for your actions
Treat yourself and others with Respect
Act with Courage every day
Act with Kindness when dealing with others

Posters with these core expectations were placed strategically throughout the schools and community, setting a tone. These placards sowed thoughts and provided visible reminders that supported prosocial behavior. A high school in another district listed their expectations under the heading "This is What We Stand For." I think that sentiment captures the true intent of defining and communicating expectations.

The Social Ripple Effect is applicable to all communities. The same three groups exist. My guesstimate about the percentage of antisocial disruptors that it takes to ruin a school climate is likely to hold true for communities. Additionally, the formula for improvement remains relevant. We need the majority of responsible citizens to rally around shared expectations and principles, then actively support one another.

Black neighborhoods suffer the most from antisocial disruptors. This is not racist; it is a depressing truth. Listen to the many stories about "how tough it is to make it out of the hood" or "how many friends have been killed or landed in prison." Incarceration rates are not driven by racism—they are in direct proportion to the percentage of antisocial disruptors in a given community. As proof, go back to the prisoners' communities and examine the quality of life in their neighborhoods. Look at the houses, the schools, and the level of commercial enterprise as a starting point. Ask grandmothers if they feel comfortable walking down their street, if they feel safe in their home, and if they are optimistic about their grandchildren's future. This is not the effect of "white privilege;" it is the impact of *antisocialism* degrading the quality of life. Listen to antisocial thug rap lyrics that resonate through the minds of youth in these areas and examine the results. These raps are not words of social protest; they are immoral directives that lead to personal and social misery.

## CORNERSTONES OF PROSOCIAL COMMUNITIES

Components of good citizenship can be drawn from any number of sources. The *McGuffey Readers* did an outstanding job in this area. We can also look at the findings from the educator survey of student behavior and the constructive elements of the *Prosocial Hierarchy*. Popular approaches to character education outline qualities that help individuals lead successful lives. Thomas Lickona's *Educating for Character* stresses the importance of respect and responsibility. *Character Counts!* emphasizes "Six Pillars of Character," which are trustworthiness, respect, responsibility, fairness, caring, and citizenship. William Bennett's *Book of Virtues* discusses responsibility, courage, compassion, loyalty, honesty, friendship, persistence, hard work, self-discipline, and faith.

When I ask educators to list the qualities needed to enhance their school climate, *respect* and *responsibility* dominate the list—no contest. The difficulty with these two concepts is that they are general and abstract. After going through the process of developing expectations with many schools and giving a great deal of thought to what works well, I settled on the *Cornerstones of Prosocial Communities* shown below: Manners, Kindness, Courage, and Self-Control.

## CORNERSTONES OF PROSOCIAL COMMUNITIES

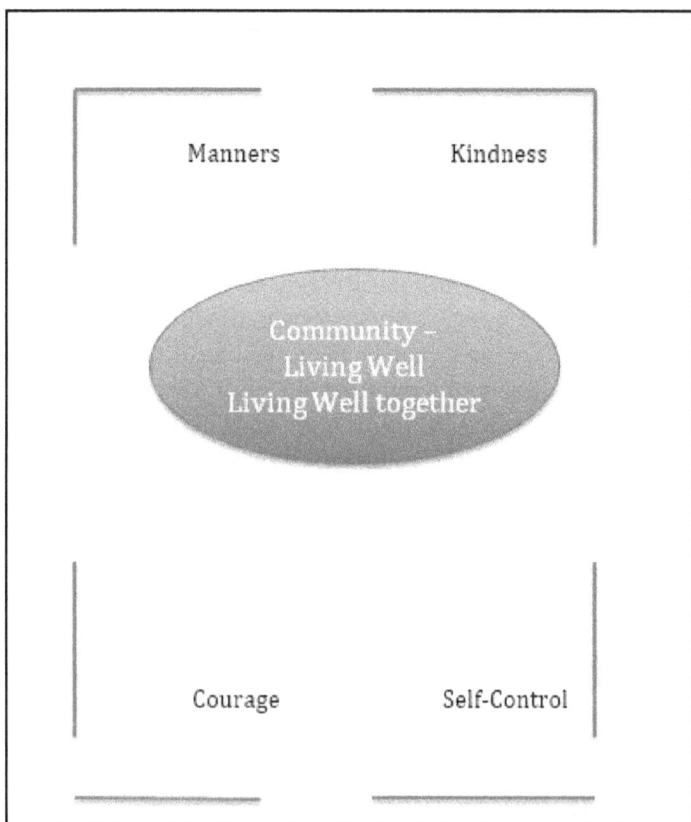

Manners     Kindness

Community –
Living Well
Living Well together

Courage     Self-Control

I selected these four qualities because manners and kindness are concrete manifestations of respect. They establish a tone for how we interact with others. They build connections that make life pleasant. Self-control and courage are elements of responsibility. Self-control and the ability to delay gratification are essential for individuals to succeed in the world. They are the foundation of emotional intelligence. Courage has many manifestations. My wife, Nancy, and I wrote the following article about courage:

## APPRECIATE EVERYDAY COURAGE
### Jerry and Nancy McMullen

*"Too much work, too little time!"*
*"Too much traffic!"*
*"Too much crime!"*
*"Not enough money, too many bills!"*
*"Too much pressure!"*
*"Too many ills!"*

As we enter the new millennium, few would disagree that we live in stressful times. In addition to the burdens that impact daily living, our collective awareness of problems ranging from the weather to ethnic cleansing is heightened by unprecedented access to information through print media, radio, television, and the internet. How can we manage the responsibility of balancing schedules, checkbooks, and family needs, while worrying about safety, burgeoning world population, global warming, and international politics? Among the qualities needed to function successfully in today's fast-paced and challenging world is courage.

Courage seems like an old-fashioned term, commonly associated with acts of heroism during times of crisis or conflict. This view places courage in the realm of exceptional behavior in response to dramatic events. In reality, courage is defined as mental or moral strength to venture, persevere, and withstand danger, fear, or difficulty. There are no limitations on courage pertaining to time and circumstance. Courage is more constant than intermittent, more commonplace than exceptional. It enhances our lives by enabling us to face adversity, persevere, and maintain a positive attitude.

Life presents challenges; adversity touches everyone's life in varying degrees of frequency and severity. Whether it's struggling with work, interpersonal relationships, finances, illness, or survival, no one is immune from hardship. Courage provides the will and the strength to function in the presence of adversity.

For any endeavor, there is a risk of failure. Sometimes we fail because of personal limitations; sometimes, the magnitude of the task, the competition, or even bad timing impedes success. We all suffer failures, minor or major, throughout our lives. The important issue is how we choose to deal with failure. We can quit, display anger, wallow in disappointment, or we can persevere. It is courage that fuels our ability to persist despite obstacles and frustration.

Nothing impacts perception more than attitude. Attitude is the lens through which we filter reality. A negative attitude makes us cynical, pessimistic, and obstinate. Our world shrinks as we sidestep opportunities and negate relationships. Conversely, a courageous attitude is positive, optimistic, and engaged. Life is colored by enthusiasm and hope, increasing our ability to capitalize on opportunities and build friendships.

Courage is not relegated to heroes; it is a quality that each of us possesses. According to Edwin Osgood Grover, "Courage is the stuff of which heroes are made. It is also one of the controlling qualities in the most commonplace lives. No one can live cheerfully and helpfully without living courageously. The quality of our courage largely determines the character of our lives." It is essential to recognize and appreciate the quiet "everyday courage" required to face our daily tasks amid the challenges, fears, and difficulties that punctuate ordinary life.[3]

## EXERTING FREE WILL

It is important to understand that our lives are impacted not only by nature and nurture, but also by free will. We are capable of acting in accordance with an ethical/moral standard that is independent from external forces and circumstances. Willpower fuels our uniquely human capacity to reason and choose what we do. As Reid noted, "Moral Liberty does not merely consist of the power of *doing what we will*, but in the power of *willing what we will.*" To summarize this in a visual format, I offer the following reminder. Being a good citizen means clarifying our values, stopping to deliberate, then using our will power to make good choices.

# GOOD CITIZENSHIP

STOP

THINK

MAKE A
GOOD CHOICE

# CHAPTER 3

# CASE STUDY: SADLY, MICHAEL BROWN DIED LIVING HIS LYRICS

Michael Brown's death was a tragedy that triggered a series of upheavals, including mass destruction in Ferguson, Missouri, riots around the country, and killing of police officers. Events in Ferguson spawned slogans such as "Hands up, don't shoot" and "Black Lives Matter" that were given standing in the 24–7 news cycle. These chants morphed into blatant anti-white sentiment that loathes "white privilege." The mainstream media broadcasts such refrains without systematic analysis. The influence of their headlines and sound bites is powerful.

This chapter uses the Michael Brown-Darren Wilson altercation as a case study to investigate suppositions associated with these slogans. I will focus on three elements: 1) Michael Brown's school, Normandy High—I start here because schools are representative of their surrounding communities. To understand any person, it is always beneficial to look at the context in which they operate. 2) Michael Brown's character—the best way to gain insight regarding a person's character is to review their thoughts and actions. The most public information in these areas are Brown's rap lyrics and his behavior on the day he died. I rely on grand jury testimony for understanding the nature and sequence of events. 3) The aftermath—the final component is a look at events in and around Ferguson, Missouri, following Brown's death.

Objective ethical and social criteria are used to evaluate these elements. The ultimate goal is to discover the facts and define the problem. We cannot solve problems until they are accurately identified. We cannot provide answers if we ask the wrong questions. Our politicians and mainstream media lead us into a wilderness of misconception. We need sensible guides to find our way out.

## NORMANDY HIGH SCHOOL

Michael Brown graduated from Normandy High School. Ninety-eight percent of Normandy's student population is black. Ninety-two percent of families are at the poverty level. More than 50 percent of the student body moves at least once during the school year. The 2013 four-year graduation rate was 53 percent. Normandy flounders academically. Out of more than 500 school districts in Missouri, Normandy was one of three to lose state accreditation as a "failed district" with chronically low achievement test scores. On standardized examinations during 2012, only 22 percent of students passed communication arts and 23 percent passed math.[1] Few students take advanced courses. Office of Civil Rights data from 2011 revealed that of the 1,064 students attending Normandy High School, only four were enrolled in a calculus class and thirty-three were enrolled in physics.[2]

Elisa Crouch wrote a May 5, 2013, *St. Louis Post-Dispatch* article titled, "Normandy High: The most dangerous school in the area." She reported that behavior problems are rampant at Normandy. Disciplinary incidents doubled between 2009 and 2012. The overall suspension rate of 27.8 per 100 students was second highest in the state. It seems ironic that the only school in Missouri with a higher rate of reported incidents in 2012 was Kansas City's Central Academy of Academic Excellence. Infractions at Normandy included assaults, drugs, and weapons.[3]

Crouch reported that Normandy High struggles "with a culture of violence" in which as many as five fights erupt in hallways and classrooms in a given day. Teacher Dawn Baldesi, who was pepper-sprayed by a student while breaking up a fight between girls, explained, "Teaching is very difficult. Teachers get cussed out, yelled at. There are so many write-ups you can't keep up." By April 1, 2013, police and fire crews were called to Normandy High eighty-three times, responding to repeated fires in trashcans and custodial closets. Fire Chief Quinten Randolph said students were "setting the toilet paper on fire. They were setting the soap dispensers on fire. They were setting old papers, books on fire under the stairwells." The district conducted a "community conversation" on school safety at Barack Obama Elementary School. Approximately 20 people attended; most of them were not parents. Superintendent Stanton Lawrence, who was leaving the district at the end of the school year, lamented a total of 1,729 suspensions during 2012; 285 of these were severe infractions resulting in ten-day out-of-school suspensions.[4]

Mayhem also takes place at the middle school, where Normandy Chief of Police Frank Mininni said his department responds as many as four times a day to handle conflicts. Mininni commented, "Any act of violence is going to trigger a response, and you don't know what that response is going to be." In an effort to reduce the violence, Normandy School District spent $1.1 million for security guards during the 2011–12 school year—and the beat goes on.[5]

Serious incidents in Normandy School District included the following events:

- On Oct. 21, 2011, Damontae Woods, 18, suffered a heart rupture in an encounter with security officer James Walls after being caught loitering in the hallway and being late to class. Woods' lawyer, Bob Herman, alleged that Walls chased Woods outside, tackled him to the asphalt, drove a knee to his chest, and handcuffed him. Woods sued the district for actual and punitive damages.[6]

- On Dec. 26, a nineteen-year-old was hospitalized after being hit in the head with a gun in Viking Hall during the Normandy holiday basketball tournament.

- On March 12, four males—three of them Normandy High School students—were arrested after a parent saw them exchanging guns in the school parking lot.

- On November 7, 2012, a sixty-four-year-old substitute teacher, Stanley Covington, was accused of placing a knife against the chest of a student and threatening to stab him. Covington said he left the classroom to get a security guard after a student threw a calculator that hit him in the head. When he returned, he said a student had taken the knife from his bag and placed it on his desk to intimidate him. Students said Covington pulled the knife from his bag, placed it against the student's chest and "threatened to cut him."[7]

- On December 3, 2012, the parent of a middle school student struck the school district's director of security with his car after being told not to park near the school buses.

- On April 11, 2013, freshman Marquez Oliver died after a classmate punched him in the chest, sending him into cardiac arrest.[8]

Student and parent reactions to Normandy's school climate included the following statements:

Daija'h Jackson, who was attacked in the hallway by a group of girls, said, "It's not a safe environment."

Three students ganged up on Ta'Darrian Floyd and bloodied his nose. He explained, "It was hard to learn, knowing that any moment I could be attacked."

His mother stated, "I sent my son there to be educated, not to be assaulted or beat up."

Charlotte Hood applied to send her son to a private school after he observed fifteen fights at school in a single week. She said, "The frequency is too much."

Carmen Clemons had two teenage sons who took advanced-placement classes. One wanted to be an engineer and his brother wanted to be a firefighter. They were "jumped" and beaten up on the fifth day of school. Ms. Clemons reported, "We've worked so hard to raise respectful kids. My boys are such good students, but my son came home terrified when another student said, 'If I see those shoes on your feet, I'm gonna take them.'" The family began exploring private schools and looking for scholarship money. [9]

The plight of the Clemons boys exemplifies what former basketball star Charles Barkley called a "dirty little secret" in the black community. He made the following statements about this issue:

"There are a lot of black people who are unintelligent, who don't have success. It's best to knock a successful black person down 'cause they're intelligent, they speak well, they do well in school, and they're successful. It's crabs in a barrel. We're the only ethnic group that says, 'Hey, if you go to jail, it gives you street cred'."

"The concept of 'crabs in a barrel' isn't new, and it's universal. If you've ever seen a bucket of crabs at the market, the ones at the bottom will try to pull down the crabs that are closer to the top."

"I lived this, and if it weren't for my parents I wouldn't have pushed through it."

"Unfortunately, as I tell my white friends, we as black people, we're never going to be successful not because of you white people but because of other black people. When you're black, you have to deal with so much crap in your life from other black people. It's a dirty, dark secret; I'm glad it's coming out."

"For some reason we're brainwashed to think if you're not a thug or an idiot, you're not black enough. If you go to school, make good grades, speak intelligent and don't break the law, you're not a good black person. . . . It's a dirty dark secret. I hate to bring white people into our crap, but as a black person, we all go through it when you're successful."[10]

Kareem Abdul-Jabbar shared the following experience about enrolling in a predominantly black Catholic school outside of Philadelphia in the 1950s:

*It was my first time away from home, my first experience in an all-black situation, and I found myself being punished for doing everything I'd ever been taught was right. I got all A's and was hated for it; I spoke correctly and was called a punk. I had to learn a new language simply to be able to deal with the threats. I had good manners and was a good little boy and paid for it with my hide.*[11]

The personal stories of Charles Barkley, Kareem Abdul-Jabbar, and the Clemons boys illustrate why it is difficult to flourish "in the hood." Addressing such issues is where groups concerned about the quality of black lives should invest their time and energy.

### Analysis and Commentary Regarding Normandy High School

Use the *Prosocial Hierarchy* to assess student behavior and its effect at the personal and social levels in the Normandy schools.

## PROSOCIAL HIERARCHY

| LEVEL | BEHAVIOR | Personal Outcome | Social Outcome |
|---|---|---|---|
| **PROSOCIAL** | MORAL CONDUCT | Character | Cohesion |
| | INITIATIVE | Achievement | Progress |
| **NEGOTIATION** | COOPERATION | Belonging | Teamwork |
| | OPPOSITION | Stress | Tension |
| **ANTISOCIAL** | DEFIANCE | Hostility | Conflict |
| | VIOLENCE | Danger | Chaos |

In schools like Normandy High, it is often a matter of "bail out or burn out" for staff. The continuous social, emotional, and physical assaults take a tremendous toll. Superintendent Lawrence estimated that about 25 percent of students caused 100 percent of the problems in Normandy School District. This percentage of disruptors is enough to sink any educational ship. The tragedy is that the majority of kids who would like to do well (we might assume 75 percent by his estimate) are robbed of opportunity. Their "right to rise" is kneecapped by antisocial classmates. There is simply too much opposition, defiance, and violence to sustain educational continuity. No progress can be made because positive initiatives are scuttled.

Don't blame the educational system for Normandy's woes; look at the perpetrators. More funding is not the answer; good citizenship is. Confrontations, fights, and fires create chaos. Each of these acts represents a choice. Normandy's loss of accreditation is emblematic of social deterioration. This is true oppression. It is not imposed by privileged "haves" on vulnerable "have nots." It is self-inflicted. Unfortunately, this pattern too often characterizes schools in predominantly black communities.

In the Philadelphia area, the same issues plague school districts such as Camden and Chester Upland that are demographically similar to Normandy. We cannot generalize about America's schools, because there is dramatic contrast among school districts. I have worked in settings where the primary behavior problem with middle school students is running in the hallways. And here's the reason for this "misbehavior"—they didn't want to be late for class. This represents a set of first principles that values education, responsibility, and initiative. It is no secret that education is important to economic success, and work habits for a lifetime are formed in school.

To create a positive climate in any school (or community), it is essential to establish expectations that are clearly defined and consistently communicated. One definition of a problem identifies it as the difference between actions or events and expectations. There are two ways to alleviate such problems—elevate behavior or lower expectations. If we truly believe in our expectations, we should not waver. We lose direction and stunt growth when we compromise our principles.

My success working with challenged schools has been highly variable. Where there is a strong principal who is willing to work with his or her staff and be an active problem-solver, results are consistently good. On the other hand, there are educators who tell me it is foolish to think that expectations like manners, kindness, courage, and self-control can be established here, because "You don't understand where these students are coming from." I do understand. This isn't rocket science. Too often their lives are compromised by dysfunctional homes, drugs, alcoholism, violence, sexual abuse, lack of father figures, multiple children from different boyfriends, incarcerated parents, negative peer pressure, damaged central nervous systems as the result of prenatal exposure to drugs or alcohol, and the instability of changing schools and classmates multiple times during a school year.

Of course I know where these students come from and the issues they face. I also know where it leads if expectations are lowered and prosocial behavior is not instilled and reinforced. Schools with the attitude of "necessity" never improve. In this view, outside forces rule the day. These schools never establish a foundation that lifts students from *what is* to *what ought to be*. Establishing first principles that allow children to form habits that are necessary to become successful in life is common sense, not naiveté.

Stories from these troubled schools tell a sordid tale. My most heart-breaking experience was with a middle school in Philadelphia. This school had the same types of problems as Normandy High. Its climate was marred by violence, disrespect, vandalism, and poor academic performance. A girl had been raped in the classroom in the presence of a substitute teacher. There were fatal shootings outside the building. I was called to help establish a behavior management program that would improve school climate and student responsibility.

The first indicator that I would be unsuccessful was the black principal's refusal to take part in the training. She was too preoccupied arranging for work to be done on her vacation home in Atlantic City to join her staff. The guidance counselor was ineffective and appeared to view her primary role as placing posters about "Respect" and "Responsibility" at key points in hallways. Teachers felt frustrated and unsupported. They were particularly disturbed by the principal's review of every student's report card before it went home. During her review, she changed all *Fs* and *Ds* to *Cs*, because she did "not want to harm any student's self-esteem." In a perverted effort to increase self-esteem, she rendered the values of cooperation, initiative, and perseverance meaningless. What teacher worth their salt would want to work for her? Her teachers developed the strategy of locking their doors (to ward off the hall crawlers) and keeping their students shielded in order to survive. As soon as the opportunity arose, they took jobs in other schools or school districts, or they left education.

The custodian in this school was a black man who grew up in the neighborhood and was committed to the students and community. He served as an active and effective role model. He greeted students by name and went out of his way to provide structure and support. He finally resigned when he became too frustrated with the relentless vandalism (such as breaking sinks, toilets, soap dispensers and setting fires around the building). His departure was sad, representing another loss in the downward spiral. These educationally deprived students were victims caught in a maelstrom that cripples too many schools in black communities.

Who is responsible for the dysfunction in black schools? Jason L. Riley suggests two underlying causes in his book, *Please Stop Helping Us: How Liberals Make It Harder for Blacks to Succeed.* He lists the high percentage of fatherless homes as a prime candidate, noting that, "more than 70 percent of black children are born to unwed mothers. Only 16 percent of black households are married couples with children, the lowest of any racial group in the United States."[12]

Riley says another contributing element is coarsening of the larger black culture. Gangsta rap is a prime contributor in this area. Riley stated, "Rappers have long expressed pride in spreading degeneracy among black youths. 'You walk into a fourth or fifth grade black school today,' Chuck D of Public Enemy told the *Village Voice* in 1991, 'I'm telling you, you're finding chaos right now 'cause rappers come in the game and threw that confusing element in it, and kids say like, 'Yo, f*ck this'."[13] My observations suggest that Chuck D is correct too often. Sadly, he demonstrates no moral conscience for promoting the "Yo, f*ck this" attitude toward authority and education that undermines the destiny of youth. Outcomes associated with this mindset are dreadful.

Riley also decries Barack Obama's approval of rap. During a 2010 *Rolling Stone* interview, Obama expressed his affinity for rappers like Jay Z and Lil Wayne.[14] Jay Z's pre-2010 titles include, *Big Pimpin, Threat*, and *B\*tches and Sisters*. Lil Wayne's pre-2010 titles include *My Nigga, Pussy Monster, Dick Pleaser*, and *Always Strapped*. These performers, for whom Obama has an affinity, promote misogyny, drug dealing, and violence. Youth listen to these performers and adopt them as role models. We come back to a fundamental truth; good citizenship produces good schools while antisocialism breeds havoc.

## MICHAEL BROWN AND HIS LYRICS

The mainstream media never examined Michael Brown's personal history in detail. What were his habits? What was he like in school? How did he spend his time? Why was he bouncing from house to house and not living with his mother? What conflict did he have with his grandmother before storming out? There was a lot that we did not know. The media shied away from unflattering information because they feared being labeled racist. Brown often was pictured in his cap and gown, giving the impression of a young scholar.

John Elgon, a thirty-one-year-old black reporter for the *New York Times*, wrote the most objective and balanced review. He reported these positive facts about Brown: Brown overcame early struggles to graduate high school on time with the assistance of Normandy's Credit Recovery Program; he had no criminal record; he rarely got into physical altercations—when confronted "He'll swell up like, 'I'm mad,' and you'll back off" because of his size; he rapped glowingly about his stepmother; and, during the final weeks of his life "he was grappling with life's mysteries," speaking seriously about religion and the Bible after seeing a cloud formation that he interpreted as "Satan chasing the angel and the angel running into the face of God."[15]

On the other side, Elgon reported less flattering facts: Brown was caught on a security camera stealing cigars and bullying the clerk in a convenience store; he left McCluer High School in ninth grade after being accused of stealing an iPod; his father reported that "his grades were kind of edgy, that's why I said I had to keep my foot on his neck to keep him on track;" and, he occasionally smoked marijuana and drank alcohol. In the last year of his life he began producing rap songs that included violent themes. His cousin, Bryan Douglas, stated, "for his music he adopted a persona to appeal to hip-hop fans." The night before his death Brown posted the following Facebook message: "Everything happen for a reason. Just start putting 2 n 2 together. You'll see it."

Playing off the angel in the clouds anecdote, Eligon commented that Michael Brown "was no angel." (I believe most of us would have no difficulty confessing that we are not angels; and, I'd be willing to lead the way to the confessional.) In the current socio-political climate, this comment drew criticism from activists and journalists and the *New York Times* wilted under the criticism. Both Eligon and editor Margaret Sullivan apologized, saying, "That choice of words was a regrettable mistake." *Times* national editor Alison Mitchell appeared to take a firmer, more objective stance. She commented, "The story basically says he's human. If you read the full profile, it's a sensitive, nuanced account of this young man."[16]

Michael Brown's parents and their lawyer snarled at anyone mentioning the videotape of him robbing a convenience store and strong-arming the clerk, decrying "character assassination." They railed at anything remotely critical. If Martin Luther King was serious about judging people on the content of their character rather than the color of their skin, a more detailed examination of Brown's thoughts and actions is needed. The best examples of his thoughts around the time of his death are gleaned from the rap messages posted on his SoundCloud page. These lyrics are readily available on the internet. Articles such as those written by Jim Hoft[17] and Doug Giles[18] present excerpts and direct links to these postings. Michael Brown explained, "I write all my lyrics down as I go off the top of my head."[19] We also may conclude these words represented a mindset that guided his actions on the day he died.

Brown's lyrics are a bit garbled and his line of thinking tangential; however, the following excepts provide a sense of his attitude and orientation:

*My niggas from the area, we don't play . . .*

*On my side of town, when the sun go down, you in trouble now . . .*

*You f\*ck with niggas,*
*They don't even give a f\*ck about you . . .*

*With this Glock in your face,*
*and you betta not make a sound,*
*and I only like White men on my money . . .*
*Those who are last shall be first,*
*Whites on the bottom . . .*

*You know we rock,*
*Lil Vee, I keep the Glock,*
*With 30 shots . . .*

*My favorite part is when they hit the ground.*
*I soak em up like I'm ringin' out a sponge . . .*

*. . . gotta get mine, no nine to five, 'til I die . . .*

*I'll be countin' money by myself.*
*I'm a rich nigga, so I got that wealth.*
*I f\*ck three [?] hos by myself. While I'm smoking on this . . .*

*Every time I call your B\*tch I make her cum.*
*And when she cums I'm cummin all over her tush.*
*I beat that pussy up and then be on the run.*
*I roll fat blunts they look just like my thumb. . .*

This Brown rap mimics the "Bad Boys" theme song used for the *Cops* television show:

*Shit talka, shit talka whatcha gonna do,*
*When a real killa, killa come for you . . .*
*Let me live my life, I just want some money . . .*
*Take you out in a flash of my bullet . . .*
*All they heard was the blast . . .*

These excerpts are not cherry-picked to make a point. They are examples of Michael Brown's mindset and the gangsta persona he adopted. Those desiring a more detailed perspective should listen to them in their entirety. *Time* magazine never put these lyrics on the cover nor did they devote an issue to the destructive impact gangsta rap on the lives of black youth.

## ANALYSIS AND COMMENTARY REGARDING MICHAEL BROWN'S RAP LYRICS

The goal for those seeking objectivity in race relationships should be to analyze thoughts and behavior without regard to their source. Some common sense questions that have relevance for evaluating the lyrics written "off the top of his head" include the following: Who identifies as a nigga? Who makes blanket threats to harm people coming to their side of town? Who declares they don't give a f*ck about you and thrusts a pistol in your face? Who says that one race should be on the bottom? Who refers to police as "shit talkas," then describes themself as a "real killa" taking out cops "in a flash of my bullet?" Make an objective judgment. If you had to guess, what is this person's destiny? Remove race-colored lenses. Use Pojman's four moral/ethical components as the starting point for analysis:

| | |
|---|---|
| Behavior or acts | that may be right, wrong, or permissible |
| Consequences | that are good, bad, or indifferent |
| Character | that is virtuous or vicious |
| Motives | that are based on good will or bad will |

Brown's raps dwell on behavior that is clearly antisocial. Violence, threat, intimidation, racism, misogyny, and threats directed at police are prominent themes. The portrayed character is vicious. The motives emanate from ill will. There is no moral conscience. No good can emerge for anyone acting on these thoughts.

Michael Brown adopted a persona learned from a coarse culture. The scope and sequence of this instruction was rooted in the messages of gangsta rap. Although there are many participants in this genre, I'll only mention Niggaz wit Attitudes (NWA) because they were early and influential contributors. Formed in 1986, they continue to draw attention through a popular 2015 film telling a Hollywood version of their story.

*Niggaz wit Attitudes.* NWA, pioneers in popularizing gangsta rap, bragged they were the "world's most dangerous group." They made a fortune, selling more than ten million units in the United States. Their second album, *Niggaz4Life*, was the first hardcore rap album to debut at number one on the Billboard 200 sales chart. The group ranked eighty-third on *Rolling Stone's* "100 Greatest Artists of All Time." A biopic about the group, *Straight Outta Compton*, was released during August 2015 and reportedly grossed more than $200 million worldwide. During December, 2015, it was announced they would be 2016 inductees into the Rock and Roll Hall of Fame.[20]

NWA hyped thug principles that continue to have tremendous impact in the black community—and beyond. Their titles include *Real Niggaz, F*ck tha Police,*

*Gangsta Gangsta, Niggaz4Life, Real Niggaz Don't Die, Appetite for Destruction, A B\*tch is a B\*tch, One Less B\*tch*, and *Findum F\*ckum & Flee* (that is not the name of their law firm). Reading their lyrics—which are readily available on internet sites including metrolyrics.com—provides insight regarding their moral code. In line after line, rap after rap, they profanely glorify violence, threat, intimidation, racism, misogyny, and hatred of police. Read their lyrics and rate them for yourself on a scale from one to ten to determine where they fit in terms of moral versus immoral; virtuous versus vicious; and, prosocial versus antisocial. The following are story lines and lessons taught by NWA.

*Real Niggaz* establishes an operational definition for what it takes to be a nigga: A) refer to yourself, your friends, and all other blacks as niggas; B) be extremely materialistic; c) never complete a sentence that does not contain at least one of the following words - f\*ck, motherf\*cker, dick, or nigga; D) become physically violent at the slightest provocation; E) don't care about others and try to instill fear in those around you with threats of violence; and, F) show no reluctance to kill another person—in fact, celebrate the possibility and the fact.

*F\*ck tha Police* is one of NWA's most popular numbers. It repeatedly chants the title, allowing the message to reverberate in the minds of its listeners. The group brags about being sneaky criminals, but become enraged when their acts bring them into contact with authorities of law and order. Any contact with police is resented as an act of social injustice, qualifying NWA as members of the victim class. They describe themselves as armed, dangerous, and more than willing to kill police officers whom they designate as punks.

NWA's repulsive misogynistic orientation is captured in *A B\*tch Iz A B\*tch* and *One Less B\*tch*. In the former number, they establish a behavioral standard in which women are verbally demeaned before being physically abused. In *One Less B\*tch*, they tout their self-identity as the "world's most dangerous group." Then they go into explicit detail about gang raping a prostitute before killing her with a .44 caliber handgun. This murder was committed to demonstrate the perpetrator is a "real nigga." The next victim is a district attorney's wife who is murdered so she couldn't aggravate the nigga. A bullet in the chest kills another prostitute. The rap ends with a double murder when NWA comes home and finds a nigga on the couch with his b\*tch. All this killing is celebrated with repeated chants in the chorus. The *Washington Post* declared that NWA's album displayed "a psychotic, brutal and obsessive fixation on beating, raping and killing groupies and prostitutes that would baffle even Sigmund Freud. Dr. Dre, Eazy-E and M.C. Ren spend the entire second half of their otherwise masterfully produced album verbally reducing women to a subhuman level." In a perverse display of values, the author of this article, Gil Griffin, legitimizes the "raw edge" of NWA's behavior as an accurate representation of "the anger and frustration of many disenfranchised urban blacks who suffer from virulent racism and abject poverty."[21] This conclusion represents the *Washington Post's* moral perspective, circa 1991.

An August 8, 1991, *Rolling Stone* article by Alan Light provides insight regarding the group. He interviewed them after their second album, *Efil4zaggin* debuted at number two on the *Billboard* album chart. Light said his interview took place at the "sunny, alarmingly professional offices" of their Ruthless Records label in "the meticulous suburban office park outside Los Angeles." Group member Easy posed the question, "How can some motherf*ckers with a street record get Number One over motherf*cking AC/DC, Paula Abdul, and all that shit?" Easy went on to explain, "When we first started, everybody was black this, black that, the whole positive black thing. We said f*ck that—we wanted to come out in everybody's face." [22] Their insidious goal was to undermine that "positive black thing." Is it any wonder that schools like Normandy struggle to maintain order and enroll students in advanced courses? NWA provides an immoral potion that poisons minds and destroys lives.

Proving that NWA live their lyrics, group member Dre physically assaulted Dee Barnes, the black hostess of the show *Pump It Up*, because he didn't like her presentation of a dispute between the group and former member Ice Cube. According to Barnes, Dre picked her up and "began slamming her face and the right side of her body repeatedly against a wall near the stairway." After Dre tried to throw her down the stairs and failed, he began kicking her in the ribs and hands. She escaped and ran into the women's rest room. Dre followed her and then "grabbed her from behind by the hair and proceeded to punch her in the back of the head."[23]

In the *Rolling Stone* article, Dre offered the following analysis of his behavior: "People talk all this shit, but you know, if somebody f*cks with me, I'm gonna f*ck with them. I just did it, you know. Ain't nothing you can do now by talking about it. Besides, it ain't no big thing—I just threw her through a door." Other NWA members expressed their agreement. Ren said, "She deserved it – b*tch deserved it." Eazy added, "Yeah, b*tch had it coming." And Ren confirmed, "Coming like a motherf*cker, she shouldn't have done that." Barnes said, "Their whole philosophy has been that they're just telling stories, just reporting how it is on the streets. But they've started believing this whole fantasy, getting caught up in their press, and they think they're invincible. They think they're living their songs."[24]

We've seen the influence of NWA's messages in the high-profile behavior of National Football League players and other athletes. They are multi-millionaires, but their moral compass is set by gangsta principles. The reverberating lyrics turn emotions into abusive behavior toward women.

Remember Minnich's description of the powerful content in *McGuffey's Readers?* He noted: "Each day the dawn of a widening world opened word by word, poem by poem, oration by oration, essay by essay, until the whole realm of earth's worthy spirits became companion to his thoughts." Gangsta rap has an equally powerful impact. Word by word, line by line, rap by rap, they expose listeners to thoughts that are profane, vile, and antisocial. Those who assimilate these messages are socially and morally degraded. The body count is huge. The fiscal cost is staggering. The amount of heartache imposed on good people is obscene.

Take a moment to compare Michael Brown's lyrics with those of NWA. They are mirror images. Michael Brown lapsed into a cultural persona characterized by defiance and violence. He paid a terrible price. He died living his lyrics.

Barack Obama and Eric Holder devoted a tremendous amount of time and federal resources examining and discussing issues surrounding Michael Brown's death. The "Obama Finger of Blame" pointed directly at police and their insensitivity to and harassment of "communities of color." Bias and injustice were the recurring themes. Consciously or subconsciously, he validated the NWA principle of loathing police. Concerns about thug principles and the behavior they promote never entered his message.

Common sense shows the devastation resulting from gangsta behavior. Homicide rates for 2015 showed 119 murders in Washington, DC, 277 in Philadelphia, and 340 in Baltimore. Every one of these deaths represents a personal story and a loss for family and friends. In worst-case scenarios, innocents are caught in the crossfire and children die. Too many black neighborhoods are war zones, and police have to step into the fog of war in an attempt to instill order. If Black Lives Matter wants to commit to a vital cause, they should dedicate themselves to intervening and helping in these neighborhoods and schools. Help is needed. The work is hard.

## THE EVENTS OF AUGUST 9, 2014, GRAND JURY TESTIMONY

The following information comes from the *State of Missouri v. Darren Wilson Grand Jury Transcript.* Robert McCulloch was prosecutor of record, and Assistant Prosecuting Attorneys Kathi Alizadeh and Shelia Whirley worked the case for St. Louis County. I cite a considerable amount of testimony verbatim to assure witness voices are heard.

Two central figures offered differing versions of what happened on the day Michael Brown died. Brown's companion, Dorian Johnson, shared one version.

His comments were widely broadcast, creating a national uproar and generating slogans such as "Hands up, don't shoot" that were endorsed and amplified by the media. The second key figure was Officer Darren Wilson. His explanation received much less attention and gravitas from mainstream media and politicians. I present both sides of the story.

I summarize forensic evidence presented by expert witnesses to establish an objective base for understanding the events as well as the rationale for the grand jury's decision. There were many witnesses with a wide range of credibility—including admitted liars. Those looking for an overview should read Kevin O'Connell's book, *The Case for Probable Cause: A Study of the Darren Wilson/ Michael Brown Grand Jury Decision*. Only two additional witnesses will be presented here: Viron, the friend Michael Brown was living with during the last weeks of his life, and a mature black female considered to be one of the most credible witnesses. The grand jury investigation began on August 20, 2014, eleven days after Michael Brown's death.

## DORIAN JOHNSON'S GRAND JURY TESTIMONY

*Grand Jury Transcript of September 10, 2014*, pp. 5–176. Dorian Johnson was the twenty-two-year-old black male who was Brown's companion on the day he died. Johnson stated that he had "just (about eight months earlier) moved to those apartments, I had me and my girlfriend, my daughter, we were staying in the apartment, two bedroom apartment, I had a roommate." Johnson met Big Mike about three months prior to the incident through a mutual friend. He described Brown as a person who didn't speak a lot. Johnson himself was "working at the time of me first moving into the apartments. I recently lost my job . . . so now I'm on the verge of finding new work and finding a way to pay the bills." Brown had moved out of his grandmother's apartment following a dispute and was staying with a friend.

When asked how his day began, Johnson explained, "August the 9th, it began like any other day. I start my morning, I wake up, I take a shower, and I ask my girl does she like breakfast, what would she like for breakfast. I head out to go get it. Upon getting breakfast I get me some cigarillos. I smoke marijuana in my mornings when I start my day off, so I was going headed to the store." As he left the apartment, around seven o'clock. he ran into Michael Brown and told him that he was going for some "'rillos" and to get something to eat for "me and my girl." Brown said he would "match" Johnson, meaning that they would exchange blunts and smoke marijuana together. He said Brown proposed walking to the store to get cigarillos. When asked how long it was before they arrived at the store, Johnson said, "I mean, it wasn't really an hour it wasn't that long . . . "

Heading to the Ferguson Market (around 11:30 a.m., four-and-a-half hours later), Johnson had no reason to believe that Brown would not pay for the cigarillos. He said, "I never thought that he didn't have any money because like I said, when I did see him the times that I see him, he dressed nice and next generation clothing, so it is kind of pricier, so I figure that he had money."

Once at the Ferguson Market, Brown reached over the counter, took a box of sixty-nine-cent mini cigarillos, and handed them to Johnson. He then reached a second time and grabbed a handful of single cigarillos. As Brown made his way toward the door, Johnson "didn't see money get transferred to the store clerk and that's why I sat the box of cigarillos back on the counter. I've been to the store a lot of times." As the store clerk tried to stop Brown from leaving without paying, Johnson observed, "So at the time when he (Brown) slung the door open, I was making my way, I was trying to get around Big Mike and the store clerk to exit the store because I didn't want any part of it, I know there was cameras in the store." As he attempted to leave, there was a physical confrontation between Brown and the clerk, with Brown pushing and intimidating the clerk, who was half his size. As they walked out, Johnson heard the clerk say that he was going to call the police.

Interchanges between Kathi Alizadeh and Dorian Johnson regarding events at the Ferguson Market included the following dialogue:

Alizadeh: (There was) like a push away.

Johnson: Fast push away, and I don't know if the store clerk was going to walk back on or anything, but that was like a stare down, like he kind of like stared at him.

Alizadeh: And that was threatening, don't you think, he (Brown) is six foot five inches tall."

Johnson: He was a small man. He was almost smaller than me (Johnson described himself as five foot six or seven, weighing between 123 and 125 pounds), shorter than me, you are right.

Alizadeh: That would be extremely intimidating, don't you think?

Johnson: I could see where it made the store clerk kind of eased off . . . You know what, I will just leave this at the hands of the police.

Alizadeh: At this point, I mean, this is not behavior you are used to seeing from him (Brown), correct?

Johnson: No, ma'am, I wasn't aware of it.

Alizadeh: But it is clearly very much macho, I'm going to take these cigarillos, I know he's not saying that, but that was kind of his demeanor, like what are you going to do, stop me? I'm taking them, right?

Johnson: Correct, yes, ma'am.

Alizadeh: So, you know, when you go the store and you see him just take these cigarillos and you said he just said I'm going to take these cigarillos, right?

Johnson: Yes, ma'am, correct.

Alizadeh: That's really brash, wouldn't you agree?

Johnson: Yes, ma'am.

Alizadeh: That's like indignant. And then the clerk tries to stop him, he pushes the clerk aside?

Johnson: Yes, ma'am.

Alizadeh: Okay. So then you are walking down the street, I know you said you are kind of freaked out at this point?

Johnson: Yes, ma'am.

Alizadeh: And you see cop cars coming by oh, my God, you know, but Big Mike doesn't really care, does he?

Johnson: Not so much care because when he saw, he looked at my face. I'm just walking like oh, my goodness. When I see the squad car I kind of follow it, I want to see are they going to the store or what is going on. And once he sees that on my face, he is like just walk normal, so we are just walking . . .

Alizadeh: He owns the street right there, right, kind of?

Johnson: I don't want to say he thought he owned the street, he was very bold . . .

When asked what happened next, Johnson stated, "At that time eating and all of those other things that I had on my mind were left field. I had just witnessed something occur that I feel like if not, you know, I was there. So I walked in with him, I felt like I was an accomplice. I was trying to figure it out in my head at the time we were leaving out of the store like, all right, I didn't know this was going to happen. I didn't touch anything, but I did see what just happened and I know there was a crime."

Johnson went on to explain, "I asked him, I looked at him, actually, looked at him for a while and stared at him because the times when I did meet him before that day, he didn't strike me as a person who would do anything like that. He never talked about any crimes or anything like that. So I was asking him, I was like, you know hey, I don't do stuff like that. What's going on? And so much is giving me an answer as to why he did it was he was basically laughing it off, be cool, be calm, stuff like that laughing it off but in my head I'm like, I can't be calm, I can't be cool because I know what just happened and we were on camera." When asked if Brown's judgment was compromised by smoking marijuana, Johnson swore that neither he nor Brown smoked that morning.

It was between 11:30 a.m. and 12:00 p.m. when the two left the store and headed home. During what Johnson estimated to be a four- to five-minute walk from the market to Canfield Green Apartments, Johnson spotted a police cruiser and thought, "At that time in my head I was like, wow, he called the police. They came really quickly, I knew that they would probably come quickly. I was just, wow, we're really going to get locked up, this is going to happen. . . . They drove past. . . . He (Brown) did not put the cigarillos in his pocket. The cigarillos now he has them in both hands, now he is spreading them evenly apart and we are walking down plain sight West Florissant to Canfield."

"In my mind, I'm still trying to fathom everything that is going on and why he didn't put the cigarillos in his pocket. He still had them in his hand the whole time leaving out the store, all the way walking down Canfield Drive."

During this walk, Johnson said they engaged in casual conversation about personal things including Johnson's ability to "transform to coming from where I was and getting on track." He said, "I knew he wasn't someone like me, I knew he didn't grow up where I grew up from, where there was a bunch of violent gangs and violent stuff occurring all the time. I knew that much about because I read from his demeanor he didn't come up that way. I'm telling him about my life story and how I come up from a bunch of tragedies. I went to school, I was still able to do things that I need to do in life."

Because they were walking down the middle of Canfield Drive, a juror made the following observation to Johnson, "In my mind an act of defiance going down the middle of the street expecting cars to go around you and, you know, pay attention to you. If I see somebody in the middle of the street I'd be concerned about hitting them and really slowing down and moving over."

Johnson: "Yeah, that's correct.

The juror: "I would interpret that they are being defiant to show strength or something."

When describing the walk down Canfield Drive, Johnson said, "We are walking like thirty seconds, I'm not really on the time preference, about thirty seconds" when they are approached by a police cruiser. "When he got right directly on the side of us, the police officer Darren Wilson, when he got on the side of us he rolled his window down and he said, get on the sidewalk, but it wasn't in a polite manner, it was very rudely . . . (He said) 'get the f*ck on the sidewalk'." According to Johnson, Big Mike said nothing, while Johnson replied that they were "just a minute away from our destination, I live in Canfield and we'll be off the street closely."

Johnson went on, "We continued to walk and have our conversation, but almost a split second we heard the tires screech, and the officer, he pulled back in the truck very fast to the point at an angle if we didn't hear his tires screech, the back of his cruiser would have struck both of us or one of us because of the way he angled in reverse." Johnson added, "And Big Mike, in an instant, Big Mike was finished saying something, his door was thrust open, very complex, he thrust his door open real hard. We was so close to the door that it hit mostly Big Mike, but it hit me on my left side and it closed back on him, like real fast. Just the same speed, boom, boom, that fast."

At that point, Johnson alleged that Wilson reached out with his left hand, grabbing 6-foot-four-inch, 289-pound Mike Brown's shirt around the neck area. After some tug-of-war, Brown placed the cigarillos on the car, then put one hand on top of the cruiser and the other hand under the window, struggling to free himself from the officer's grasp. With Brown and Wilson yelling and cussing at one another, Johnson reported, "That's the beginning of my shock level. That's where I'm like, this doesn't happen every day, something is out of order here." He continued, "There wasn't any wrestling or anything like that, punches were thrown. It was more of a tug-of-war and it was very intense, very intense."

Johnson said that Wilson never lost his grip, but Brown eventually was able to turn enough to hand Johnson the cigarillos, saying, "Grab these, Bro."

The tug-of-war continued with Officer Wilson using only his left hand. "So now as he is pulling away, it is with more power, with more force. The officer is trying to pull him inside the vehicle through the window, like he's pulling him, but he's pulling away. " During the struggle, Johnson swore that Big Mike's hands never entered the vehicle.

Johnson said as the cussing and pulling continued, he heard Officer Wilson say, "I'll shoot." At that point, Johnson declared "I was praying, I was, I'm in such shock right now and firm, because when the officer pulled up and that's when I was trying to make clear people were, he's a witness, key witness. I was so victimized that people don't even know."

He continued, "He had his gun pointed towards us. I'm still standing in the doorway at the time he said I'll shoot. He was going to say it again, I'll shoot and almost, he didn't get to finish his sentence, the gun went off." Johnson claimed the "bullet traveled outside the car and struck Big Mike in the chest, or I seen blood coming from." Johnson testified, "I never saw at no point in time Big Mike's hand touch the gun or anything like that because the gun was already out drawn . . . (Big Mike) never had his fist clenched up like in a punching manner, so much as trying to grab stuff and push himself off of." Johnson said that his friend never hit Officer Wilson.

After the first shot, Johnson said that he and Brown took off running. Johnson hid behind a car. Big Mike ran past and yelled, "Keep running, Bro." About this time, Officer Wilson exited his vehicle and moved past Johnson with his weapon drawn. After passing Johnson's location, Wilson fired a second shot at Brown's back, causing Brown to jerk, stop running, and turn to face the officer. Johnson said, "At this time Big Mike's hands was up, but not so much up in the air because he had been struck already in this region somewhere on this. It was like this hands is up and this hand is kind of like down sort of."

Johnson's testimony continued, "So I could tell he was injured because this hand was a little lower than this hand. As I'm looking at him, he said I'm, he didn't say I'm unarmed per se, he said I don't have a gun, but he's still mad, he still has his angry face."

"And before he can say the second sentence or before he can even get it out, that's when the several more shots came."

"The second statement he was starting to say I, you know, he couldn't get the full sentence out before the rest of the shots hit his body. And I stood and watched face-to-face as every shot was fired and as his body went down and his body never. His body kind of just went down and fell, you know, like a step, you know what I'm saying? Like a step, his body just kind of collapsed down and he just fell."

"Shots was definitely fired while he was going down. The last shot fired he was so close to the ground, it looked like to me he was already on the ground. His knees were, he was going down, he was already down before the last shot came."

Alizadeh: So he never like got on his knees, he was just falling down?

Johnson: "He was falling."

During follow-up questioning, Alizaheh asked a number of clarifying questions. One related to the time Johnson and Brown spent together that day. He said, "We was together from seven all the way to him dying." During that four- to five-hour span, Johnson said they never smoked weed. In fact, he declared, "We never got a chance to do anything. We never got a chance to make it back to the house."

Johnson spontaneously shared personal history during the course of the interview. He mentioned several times that he has been shot. At one point he declared, "Like I said, I've been shot at before, I've been shot once before, but I've been shot at in crazy situations, walking home from school and all."

Prosecuting attorney Whirley asked, "Is there anything you want to tell us that we just didn't think to ask that you think is important, is information about this case?"

Johnson: "Yes. Regardless of everybody's opinion of me, I know a lot of speculation of my past and criminal record that I have or anything like that, that day I felt like even though the store thing had happened, I didn't feel like someone should have lost their life."

Whirley: You mentioned something, you know, the grand jurors may want to factor. You said something about a criminal record?

Johnson: Yes, because I stay watching the news and media outlets. I see they dug though years in my past to see an incident that happened in Jefferson City, but what they fail, they keep leaving out is I was a freshman in college at this time, everybody makes, you know, crazy little moves their freshman year. . . . Basically all I keep seeing is slander on my name.

Whirley: We don't want to slander you, but we just want all the information we can get. What is the nature of the thing in Jefferson City, what happened?

Johnson: There was just basically me walking with a group of kids that I knew, we were going to a YMCA to play basketball. I didn't have membership there. They actually had membership there. So we are walking through some apartments, one of the guys, you know, he grabbed a package and, you know, he ripped it open. As we are walking towards the YMCA, I see a pool guy, he sees us, but he doesn't see anything in our hand or anything like that, but he sees us walking from out of the apartments going towards the gym.

So I guess whoever's package it was, they made the call saying someone had stole something off their property or something like that.

And I guess he took it in his own mind that I just saw these guys coming out of those apartments. When they went to run the YMCA cameras to see who had just recently walked in, I did not pay to get in, even though I was supposed to. I kind of just walked right on past, go down to the gym, play basketball.

And when the police came and they ran the camera back and they saw like he didn't pay or this group right here, they came down, they grabbed basically the last group.

Whirley: Did you get charged with that?

Johnson: I did not get charged with it, I had to go to court on two charges.

Whirley: What were the charges?

Johnson: I had a false report to an officer, I had stealing charge that they were trying to see if I was the one that had stole it. I was going to court. At that time of me leaving court, I had been fed up with being stopped by off campus police and on campus police because of the stereotypical they look at people from St. Louis. And being stopped every day, being late for class and having to remake up work, I just said you know what, Jefferson City school, Lincoln University was not for me at the time. Jefferson City, they never come and get me. The warrant is a 500 miles, my lawyer reached out to them, if you are outside 500 miles.

Whirley: Fifty miles.

Johnson: Fifty miles, we are not coming to get you. I'm sure the other police officers they see that, but they always detain me and they hold me.

Whirley: You were never on probation for that?

Johnson: When I got locked up, when I had got locked up, I got to the Jefferson City probation about the stealing, I guess I was in the middle of asking the judge can I do my probation in St. Louis because I was not from Jefferson City and in the middle of that we kind of lost contact, lost communication.

Alizadeh: I just want, you had mentioned the stealing thing and then you said a false police report?

Johnson: Yes.

Alizadeh: Is that the same incident or was that a separate thing?

Johnson: That was the same incident with the officer who actually had me, he put me in the car, took me down to the station. I had both my school campus ID and my state ID in possession of me. When the officer asked me my name, I didn't say anything so much as just handed him my identification. I was mad at the time, again, I was a freshman in college, I'm kind of angry with the police, so I don't really want to say anything to them.

## DARREN WILSON'S GRAND JURY TESTIMONY

*State of Missouri v. Darren Wilson, Transcript of: Grand Jury Volume VI, September 16, 2014*, pp. 196–281.Darren Wilson worked as a police officer in the Ferguson Police Department. He is 6 feet 4 inches tall and weighs approximately 210 pounds. On August 9, 2014, he was working the 6:30 a.m. until 6:30 p.m. day shift. Between 11:00 and 11:30 a.m., he received a call to assist with a sick infant in Northwinds, a housing complex adjacent to Canfield Green Apartments. An ambulance arrived at the same time as Officer Wilson, so he returned to his vehicle and left. At this time, a call came over his radio about a theft at the local market on West Florissant. Although the call was not clear on his portable radio, he heard that a box of cigarillos was stolen and a suspect was wearing a black shirt. This was not his call. Other officers were dispatched to the scene.

As he drove his marked Chevy Tahoe police vehicle west on Canfield Drive, he observed two men walking single file along the double yellow line. He said, "The first thing that struck me was they're walking in the middle of the street. I had already seen a couple cars trying to pass, but they couldn't have traffic normal because they were in the middle, so one had to stop to let the car go around and then another car would come."

"The next thing I notice was that Brown had bright yellow socks on that had green marijuana leaves as a pattern on them."

Wilson said he stopped, and as Johnson came past his driver's side mirror he asked, "Why don't you guys walk on the sidewalk?"

Johnson kept walking but said, "We are almost to our destination."

Wilson replied, "Well, what's wrong with the sidewalk?"

Brown responded, "F*ck what you have to say."

Wilson continued, "And when he said that, it drew my attention totally to Brown. It was very unusual and not expected response from a simple request."

"When I start looking at Brown, first thing I notice is in his right hand, his hand is full of cigarillos. And that's when it clicked for me because I now saw the cigarillos, I looked in my mirror, I did a double-check that Johnson was wearing a black shirt, these are the two from the stealing." Wilson got on his radio and said, "Frank 21 I'm on Canfield with two, send me another car." Then he "placed my car in reverse and backed up and I backed up just past them and then angled my vehicle, the back of my vehicle to kind of cut them off kind to keep them somewhat contained."

"As I did that, I go to open the door and I say, hey, come here for a minute to Brown. As I'm opening the door he turns, faces me, looks at me and says, what the f*ck are you going to do about it, and shuts my door, slammed it shut."

"I then looked at him and told him to get back and he was just staring at me, almost like to intimidate me or to overpower me. The intense face he had was just not what I expected from any of this."

"I then opened my door again and used my door to push him backwards, and while I'm doing that I tell him to, get the f*ck back, and then I use my door to push him."

"He then grabs my door again and shuts my door. . . . And I see him ducking and as he is ducking, his hands are up and he is coming in my vehicle . . . I had shielded myself in this type of manner and kind of looked away, so I don't remember seeing him come at me, but I was hit right here in the side of the face with a fist."

"After he hit me then, it stopped for a second. He kind of like, I remember getting hit and he kind of like grabbed and pulled, and then it stopped. When I looked up . . . he turns like this and now the cigarillos I see in his left hand. He's going like this and he says, 'Hey man, hold these.'"

Continuing, Wilson says, "At that point I tried to hold his right arm and use my left hand to get out to have some type of control and not be trapped in my car any more. And when I grabbed him, the only way I can describe it is I felt like a five-year-old holding onto Hulk Hogan."

Wilson said he decided against using mace because he did not want to sacrifice his left hand from shielding his face. Furthermore, he doubted that he could use mace or his asp effectively in this situation. He does not carry a taser, so that wasn't an option. He reported, "And as I'm trying to open the door is when, and I can't really get it open because he is standing only maybe six inches from my door, but as I was trying to pull the handle, I see his hand coming back around like this and he hit me with this part of his right here, just a full swing all the way back around and hit me right here."

"After he did that, next thing I remember is how do I get this guy away from me? What do I do not to get beaten inside my car?"

"So the only other option I thought I had was my gun. I drew my gun, I turned. It is kind of hard to describe it, I turn and I go like this. He is standing here. I said, 'Get back or I'm going to shoot you.'"

Wilson continued, "He grabs my gun, says, 'You are too much of a pussy to shoot me.' The gun goes down into my hip and at that point I thought I was getting shot. I can feel his fingers try to get inside the trigger guard with my finger and I distinctly remember envisioning a bullet going into my leg. I thought that was the next step."

"Like I said, I was just so focused on getting the gun out of me. When I did get it up to this point, he is still holding onto it and I pulled the trigger and nothing happens, it just clicked. I pull it again, it just clicked again."

"At this point I'm like why isn't this working, this guy is going to kill me if he gets ahold of this gun. I pulled it a third time, it goes off. When it went off, it shot through my door panel and my window was down and glass flew out of my door panel. I think that kind of startled him and me at the same time."

"When I see the glass come up, it comes, a chunk about that big comes across my right hand and then I notice I have blood on the back of my hand."

Wilson stated that Brown stepped back, "And then after he did that, he looked up at me and had the most intense aggressive face. The only way I can describe it, it looks like a demon, that's how angry he looked. He comes back towards me again with his hands up."

Wilson pulled the trigger again and the gun misfired for a third time. He immediately racked the gun, dislodging a jammed cartridge, then pulled the trigger again and the gun fired. He saw Brown running away when he looked up. He then exited his vehicle and called dispatch with the message, "Shots fired, send me more cars." Wilson said that he ran past two cars then watched Brown stop running as he reached a light pole.

Wilson stated, "So when he stopped, I stopped. And then he starts to turn around, I tell him to get on the ground, get on the ground. He turns, and when he looked at me, he made like a grunting, like aggravated sound and he starts, he turns and he's coming back towards me. His first step is coming towards me, he kind of does like a stutter step to start running. When he does that, his left hand goes in a fist and goes to his side, his right one goes under his shirt in his waistband and he starts running at me."

"As he is coming towards me, I tell, keep telling him to get on the ground, he doesn't. I shoot a series of shots. I don't know how many I shot, I just know I shot it."

"I know I missed a couple, I don't know how many, but I know I hit him at least once because I saw his body kind of jerk or flenched."

"I remember having tunnel vision on his right hand, that's all, I'm just focusing on that hand when I was shooting."

"Well, after the last shot my tunnel vision kind of opened up. I remember seeing the smoke from the gun and I kind of looked at him and he's still coming at me, he hadn't slowed down."

"At this point I start backpedaling and again, I tell him get on the ground, get on the ground, he doesn't. I shoot another round of shots. Again, I don't recall how many it was or if I hit him every time. I know at least once because he flinched again."

"At this point it looked like he was almost bulking up to run through the shots, like it was making him mad that I'm shooting at him."

"And the face that he had was looking straight through me, like I wasn't even there, I wasn't even anything in his way."

"Well, he keeps coming at me after that again, during the pause I tell him to get on the ground, get on the ground, he still keeps coming at me, gets about eight to ten feet away. At this point I'm backing up pretty rapidly, I'm backpedaling pretty good because I know if he reaches me, he'll kill me."

"And he had started to lean forward as he got that close, like he was going to just tackle me, just go right through me."

"And when he gets about that eight to ten feet away, I look down, I remember looking at my sites and firing, all I see is his head and that's what I shot."

"I don't know how many, I know at least once because I saw the last one go into him. And then when it went into him, the demeanor on his face went blank, the aggression was gone, it was gone, I mean, I knew he stopped, the threat was stopped."

"When he fell, he fell on his face. And I remember his feet coming up, like he had so much momentum carrying him forward that when he fell, his feet kind of came up a little bit and then they rested. At that point I got back on the radio and said, 'Send me a supervisor and every car you got.'"

Further interviewing included the following interchange between Shelia Whirley and Darren Wilson:

Whirley: I wanted to ask you about your relationship with the residents in the Canfield Green Apartments. . . . Did you guys have a volatile, well, how can I put this? Did you not really get along well with the folks that lived in that apartment, not you personally, I mean the police in general?

Wilson: It is an antipolice area for sure.

Whirley: And when you say antipolice, tell me more?

Wilson: There's a lot of gangs that reside or associate with that area. There's a lot of violence in that area, there's a lot of gun activity, drug activity, it is just not a very well-liked community. That community doesn't like the police.

Whirley: Were you pretty much on high alert being in that community by yourself, especially when Michael Brown said, "F*ck what you say," I think he said.

Wilson: Yes, that's not an area where you can take anything really lightly. Like I said, it is a hostile environment. There are good people over there, there really are, but I mean there is an influx of gang activity in that area.

The following interchange concluded Darren Wilson's testimony:

Whirley: I was just going, if we are sort of done with your questioning, is there something that we have not asked you that you want us to know or you think is important for the jurors to consider regarding this incident?

Wilson: One thing you guys haven't asked that has been asked of me in other interviews is, was he a threat, was Michael Brown a threat when he was running away. People asked why would you chase him if he was running away now?

I had already called for assistance. If someone arrives and sees him running, another officer and goes around the back half of the apartment complexes and tries to stop him, what would stop him from doing what he just did to me to him or worse, knowing he has already done it to one cop. And that was, he still posed a threat, not only to me, to anybody else that confronted him.

## EXPERT WITNESS TESTIMONY

The following primarily consists of bulleted summaries of key evidence presented to the grand jury by expert witnesses. These are the objective facts that form the basis for evaluating the veracity of witness testimony and for the grand jury reaching a verdict. Before outling the evidence, I present a St. Louis County Police Department crime scene detective's testimony describing the nature of the crime scene. His description is from the *Grand Jury transcript of September 3, 2014*, pp. 102–188.

This detective's primary responsibility was dealing with evidence at the crime scene. He was called to the scene shortly after 1:00 p.m. While traveling to Canfield Green Apartments, he heard the police radio report "gunshots being fired near the crime scene, so I stopped and put my vest on." Upon his arrival, he saw police and emergency vehicles as well as hundreds of pedestrians. His first step was to speak with the officers in charge and complete a walk-through of scene with a sergeant from the Ferguson Police Department.

As he completed his walk-through, "Another round of gunshots were fired and extremely close proximity to the crime scene. There was obviously a large crowd reacting to that as was well as a police reaction to it. . . . I have to be able to concentrate on what I'm looking at and trying to collect, versus trying to watch the crowd behind me that's growing ever bigger and more angry by the minute."

During his investigation, "Several people had torn down the crime scene tape, run onto the scene, the gunshots being fired, the crowd would run from this building in particular from this side of the crime scene, around this building, through the parking lot to this side of the crime scene, depending on what was happening."

"The crowd at this point were starting to chant, kill the police, numerous other derogatory things towards everything about us. And we fully expected another, I don't want to use the term riot, but an outburst once we did uncover the body and begin to move it."

The following details pertain to or came from expert witnesses:

*Medical Legal Investigator for St. Louis County Medical Examiner's Office.*

- Investigates deaths that occur in the county. Serves as "the eyes and ears of the pathologist who conducts the autopsy."

- Talked with on-scene officers, examined the body, and spoke with witnesses.

- Observed there was no stippling around the critical wounds.

- Brown had no weapons.

- Found nine wounds that appeared to be gunshot wounds.

- Brown's pockets contained two lighters, two $5 bills, and a bag of what appeared to be marijuana.

*St. Louis County Police Department Crime Scene Detective #1*

- His responsibility was to document crime scene evidence by videotaping the area, marking and photographing key pieces of evidence, creating diagrams, and collecting data.

- When he examined Wilson's SUV, he found a noticeable defect on the outside of the driver's door, but no hole. There was a corresponding hole on the inside door panel.

- Glass from the driver-side window was scattered inside the vehicle.

- The distance between Wilson's vehicle and Michael Brown's body was 159 feet and 9 inches. There was no blood between the vehicle and the body, suggesting that Brown was not seriously wounded while running away. Two blood splatters were found to the far side of Brown's body near Coppercreek Court.

- Wilson's weapon, a .40 caliber Sig Sauer semiautomatic pistol, holds thirteen rounds of ammunition. Twelve spent shell casings were found at the scene. One round remained in the weapon's chamber.

- A black and yellow bracelet, a brown bracelet, and a red baseball cap were found.

*St. Louis County Police Department Crime Scene Detective #2.*

- This detective was assigned to interview Officer Wilson about the shooting of Michael Brown.

- The interview was conducted at the Ferguson Police Department in the presence of Officer Wilson's lieutenant, an attorney, and another detective.

- The interview shifted to Christian Northwest Hospital where Wilson was taken for medical examination.

- Wilson had reddening to the left and right sides of his jaw, and the right side of his jaw was swollen.

- This detective took photographs of Wilson's facial injuries and conducted a thirty-minute interview. During this interview, Wilson described events in a manner consistent with his Grand Jury testimony.

- Wilson said Brown started the fight while he was still in his vehicle. Brown swung wildly, punching him in the chin, face, shoulder and chest.

- Wilson indicated that Brown had "an intense and psychotic look on his face."

- When asked about his weapon, Wilson theorized the gun misfired because Brown's hand was over the slide or pushing down on the hammer.

*St. Louis County Police Department Detective #3.*

- This officer received a call to join the detective interviewing Wilson at Christian Northwest Hospital.

- He noted that Wilson reported pain or discomfort in his face, neck and head.

- He documented Wilson's bruises and swelling by taking fifty photographs.

- He observed bloodstains on the left leg of Wilson's uniform pants.

- There were two red stains on Wilson's gun, including the slide.

*Physician's Assistant (PA).*

- The PA, who worked as a medical care specialist at the Northwest Health Care Emergency Department, examined Wilson.

- Wilson reported jaw pain, scratches to his neck, and a minor headache.

- The PA noted redness and swelling on the right side of his face and linear marks and slight puffiness on his neck.

- Wilson reported a discomfort/pain level of six on a scale from one to ten. His injuries were consistent with those caused by being punched or scratched.

*FBI Interview with Darren Wilson.*

- Interview took place August 28, 2014.

- Purpose of the interview was to determine if Wilson had violated Michael Brown's civil rights.

- Wilson's description of events was consistent with his statement on the day of the confrontation, with some areas elaborated in response to questioning.

- Wilson said his initial approach to Brown and Johnson was non-confrontational due to his desire to go to lunch.

- He indicated that his intent when backing up his vehicle was to block Brown and Johnson's path, delaying them until backup arrived. He called for backup because he was outnumbered and because of Brown's imposing size.

- When Wilson's gun fired the first time (hitting the door panel but not injuring Brown), Brown backed off, checked himself, then resumed his assault with what Wilson described as an enraged expression.

- Brown took off running along Canfield Drive after the weapon fired a second time.

- Wilson said that he pursued Brown because he believed he was a fleeing felon who assaulted and tried to kill a police officer with his own weapon. Furthermore, he considered Brown an immediate danger to others.

- Wilson said he did not fire any shots at Brown's back as he fled.

- Once Brown stopped running and turned around, he began running toward Wilson who responded by firing his first string of shots.

- Brown's body flinched and jerked. He stopped briefly then puffed his chest and resumed the charge. Wilson said Brown was within eight feet of him when he fired the final string of shots.

- In Wilson's view, Michael Brown posed a direct threat to his life when he attacked him through the window of his vehicle, when he went after his weapon, and when he turned and charged him.

*Darren Wilson's Training Officer (TO).*

- The purpose of this interview was to obtain the training officer's view of Wilson's demeanor and performance, and to provide insight into police procedure.

- The TO provided six weeks of ride-along training for Wilson when he joined the Ferguson Police Department in 2009.

- He and Wilson worked the same shift.

- He never observed Wilson employing excessive force, demonstrating bad temper, bullying, engaging in behavior that would be considered racist, or using poor judgment.

- He was not aware of any civilian complaints regarding Wilson.

- Wilson was trained in the Use of Force Triangle. This is a reactive process where the officer's options are dictated by the actions of the suspect. The goal is to use the most appropriate level of force to gain compliance. Compliance is at the center of the triangle. The three corners represent the following behaviors: (A) Compliance—full cooperation; (B) Non-threatening resistance—lack of cooperation with no threat of physical violence from the suspect; and, (C) Threatening resistance—non-compliance that includes the threat of bodily harm on the officer.

- When confronted with situations where it is deemed necessary to fire their weapon, officers are trained to aim at the center mass to terminate the threat.

*St. Louis County Medical Examiner: First Autopsy of Michael Brown.*

- Completed by the forensic pathologist employed as an assistant medical examiner for St. Louis County's Medical Examiner's Office.

- Autopsy performed on August 10, 2014.

- Brown received eleven bullet wounds from seven bullets: two entry wounds that were tangential or graze wounds; two entry wounds to the right arm, one to the chest, and two to the head; exit wounds to the forearm, back of the upper arm, and beneath the right side of the jaw; a reentry wound to the right chest above the nipple; and, graze wounds to the lateral right area near the shoulder and to the palm and thumb of the right hand.

- There were no bullet wounds to Brown's back.

- Brown's thumb wound was the only one received at close range. This wound contained soot and stippling, indicating that his hand was within six to nine inches of the weapon when it fired. The examiner was confident this wound was sustained while Brown was in close proximity to Wilson's vehicle.

- Brown had multiple abrasions, particularly on his left elbow and left wrist.

*Forensic Pathologist Recruited by Brown's Family: Second Autopsy.*

- He worked pro-bono for Brown's family, with travel expenses paid by their attorneys.

- This autopsy was performed on August 17, 2014, after Michael Brown was already embalmed and his organs and bullets removed.

- The examination relied upon photographs and x-rays.

- He believed the muzzle of Wilson's gun was within four to five inches of Brown's hand when the thumb wound was sustained.

- Brown's head was bent forward almost parallel to the ground when the fatal shot was fired.

*Military Forensic Pathologist: Third Autopsy.*

- This autopsy was completed on August 17, 2014, at the request of the Department of Justice.

- The pathologist concurred that Brown's thumb wound was the only wound containing powder, stipple, and thermal evidence that indicates the gun was fired in close proximity.

- The two wounds to the head were the only shots that incapacitated Brown. His other wounds would have allowed full mobility.

*Toxicology Report.*

- Found the presence of twelve nanograms of Delta-9-THC, the active ingredient in marijuana, in Brown's system.

*Forensic Scientist From the St. Louis County Police Department.*

- Her job was to collect bodily fluids from the crime scene, including blood, saliva, and semen. She also examined trace evidence such as fingerprints, footprints, hair, fibers, and DNA.

- DNA samples were taken from Michael Brown's blood, and a buccal (saliva) sample was obtained from Darren Wilson.

- She gathered evidence, including dried nasal mucus found on the exterior surface of the driver-side rear door, blood stains on Wilson's pants, blood on the interior door handle of Wilson's vehicle, blood on the exterior driver-side door, blood stains on Canfield Drive near Coppercreek Court, and blood on the surface of Wilson's gun. There also were two bracelets: a yellow, black, and white rubber bracelet, and a dark brown wooden beaded bracelet.

*Drug Chemist for the St. Louis County Crime Lab.*

- The chemist's job was to analyze powders, liquids, residues, plant material, and pharmaceuticals to determine if they had controlled substances in them.

- He received a plastic bag containing plant material for analysis on August 11, 2014. He found this to be 1.589 grams of marijuana, a quantity "a little bit smaller than a baseball."

- Because there was a suspicion that Brown, Johnson, and a white construction worker may have smoked "wax," Ms. Alizadeh asked the drug chemist to describe "waxing," which is a process that involves pouring liquid butane over the marijuana so that it absorbs the resinous material, creating more concentrated THC. When the butane evaporates, a sticky substance with very high THC content (wax) remains.

- There was no definitive proof that Brown smoked wax.

*DNA Technical Leader for the St. Louis County Police Department.*
DNA testing yielded the following results:

- Michael Brown was the source of DNA from the following bodily fluids: nasal mucus found on Wilson's vehicle; blood on the vehicle's interior door handle; blood found on the exterior driver-side door; blood on Wilson's uniform pants; blood on Wilson's gun; and, two blood stains found near the intersection of Canfield Drive and Coppercreek Court on the far side of his body.

- Brown's left hand had a DNA mixture of two individuals—Brown was the major contributor and Wilson the minor contributor.

- The rubber bracelet that fell off during the physical altercation contained the DNA of both Brown and Wilson. The wooden beaded bracelet apparently belonged to Dorian Johnson.

*Facts Suggested by the Forensic Evidence.*

- The toxicology report confirmed the presence of twelve nanograms of Delta-9-THC, the active ingredient in marijuana, in Brown's system. This is more than twice the level (5 nanograms) considered to cause driving impairment in states with legalized marijuana.

- Michael Brown had money in his pocket and could have purchased cigarillos if he chose to.

- Evidence shows that Brown struck Officer Wilson.

- Wilson received several significant blows to the face.

- Brown was first wounded with his hand inside Wilson's vehicle and within inches of his weapon.

- Officer Wilson fired his weapon at Michael Brown three times. The first two shots were fired while Wilson was seated in his vehicle. The first string of shots was fired with Brown in close proximity to Canfield Drive and Coppercreek Court. The second string of shots was fired after Brown moved from the intersection and back toward Wilson.

- Brown's blood was found near the sidewalk at Coppercreek Court. He moved approximately twenty-five feet back toward Wilson before being hit by the fatal shot.

- Brown was not in a kneeling position when the fatal shot was fired; he was most likely standing with his body leaning forward.

- Officer Wilson's testimony was consistent across several interviews, including the one conducted shortly after the shooting.

## VIRON'S TESTIMONY.

This testimony is an audio recording of Viron's interview with the FBI on October 3, 2014, from *Grand Jury Volume XIII*, pp. 80–202. The FBI invited Viron (his name was revealed accidentally) for a second interview because his August 13, 2014, testimony was highly incompatible with forensic evidence.

During this re-examination, Viron confirmed that Michael Brown was one of his best friends. They went to high school together and "he was around me every day." At the time of his death, Brown was living with Viron "just about a week. His granny was in the hospital. He didn't have nowhere else to go." He explained, "every day we will go record music, play video games, everything."

During questioning, Viron recapitulated his version of events of August 9, 2014. He said, "The first shot actually woke me up. I went to the window and what I saw was the officer had a gun drawn and Michael Brown's facing him on his knees."

Viron claimed that Brown pleaded for his life, saying "Please, don't shoot."

A few seconds later, "I seen him shoot him in the head. By the time I tried to get out the house, like by the time I hit the stairs, I heard four more shots go off. By the time I got to the end, when I got to the end of the steps, I heard seven more shots."

By his account, all shots were fired while Brown and Wilson were in close proximity to Wilson's police vehicle. Viron then related, "I ran across a grass hill and said they just killed my little brother for nothing. Those were my exact words."

Viron reported he didn't sleep well the night before the shooting because he had a premonition. He said, "I knew why I was up 'cause I had an intuition, like a feeling that something was going to happen. I didn't think it was going to honestly happen to him, I knew God send me a sign and I knew something was going to happen the following day."

The FBI investigator challenged Viron's past and present testimony at several junctures. The following are examples of these interchanges.

FBI: Back when you talked to the FBI previously, that was on August thirteenth, okay, just a few days after this happened, about four days after this happened. You told them that after the officer shot Brown in the head, he shot him eight more times.

Viron: Yeah.

FBI: And you said that you saw him fire four more shots into Mike Brown's body as Mike Brown's laying there lying on the ground?

Viron: Yeah.

FBI: Today you are telling me you didn't see those shots; is that right?

Viron: More importantly I heard . . . I didn't see them, but I heard them on my way running downstairs.

FBI: A problem I have today is that back on August 13th you told the FBI that Mr. Brown had blood flowing from his shoulder or rib cage on his left side. Did you actually not see that?

Viron: I didn't see exactly where he got shot at. I said, I knew he had got shot. I heard the first shot cause he stopped and he was sitting in the middle of the street. Like I told you, with his hands in the air.

FBI: Did you actually see that or not?

Viron: No, I didn't actually see. . . . That was something that I heard. That's why you told me to tell you what I actually saw, so I'm telling you what I actually saw. Someone in the community . . .

FBI: Who told you?

Viron: I don't know. There was a whole bunch of crowds, people was telling me all type of stuff. . . . They were crying, yelling and screaming. They killed him for nothing, just everybody was outside.

The agent summarized his opinion, explaining, "There is no way I could put you on the witness stand. . . . Basically just about everything that you said on August 13th, and much of what you said today isn't consistent with the physical evidence that we have in this case. . . . I'm talking about actual physical, forensic evidence at the scene, okay."

Viron: I'm telling you what I saw from my perspective. That's why I have been brought down to tell you my perspective of what's going on.

FBI: We are here to tell you what you are saying you saw isn't forensically possible based on the evidence. . . . Virtually everything that you told the FBI on August 13th doesn't match up with the evidence. . . . The entire layout of the scene is entirely different than what you described, okay. And when you came in here today and substantially changed what you say you saw and what you claim you saw on August 13th, that leads me to believe that maybe you didn't see this. And if that's the case, you need to tell me, okay.

Viron: I tell you can I leave? I don't feel too comfortable right now. . . . I ain't feeling comfortable. . . . You are telling me I didn't see what I saw. This is not the first time that it happened, they did it to me last time I was here and try to tell me . . . If I didn't see what I saw, why for the first two or three weeks I was being harassed . . . I'm telling you all right, I'm sorry, I'm telling you what I saw, I seen the man execute my best friend.

## TESTIMONY OF VIRON TO THE GRAND JURY, VOLUME XIII, PP. 138–202

Viron testified before the Grand Jury on October 16, 2014, thirteen days after his second interview with the FBI. He said that on August 9th he was living with his pregnant sister and her two young sons in the Northwinds Apartments, which are adjacent to Canfield Green Apartments. They lived directly across the street from Michael Brown's grandmother.

Brown moved in with Viron two or three weeks earlier because, "He was going through a couple things with his family and since we was best friends, he was just with me every day staying over there." When asked why Brown was living with his grandmother, he answered, "I honestly don't know. From my understanding, him and his mother was always in tit for tat." He related that, "He was bouncing back from houses to houses. He had another grandma that lived in Pine Lawn that he was also staying with at the time. And that's where he was going to school. He actually graduated from Normandy because he lived in Pine Lawn with his daddy's mother."

Viron claimed that both Michael Brown and Dorian Johnson are his cousins. When asked about the family relationship, he explained he recently learned that his father's nephew is the father of Michael Brown's two youngest siblings. With regard to Dorian, he said, "I known him from my old neighborhood since I've been young. . . . He was basically family, like blood could not make us any more related. I grew up around him and all his brothers, so I look at him as family."

Describing the sequence of events on August 9th, Viron said that he and Brown were awake until five in the morning before he "passed out in the love seat" and Brown fell asleep on the bigger sofa. They spent the night talking. Viron said Brown "was going through a phase, but we just, mostly we did a whole lot of talking that night. We did a whole lot of talking about God, just about the problems that we've been going through. We just did a whole lot of talking. Because the cable was off at that time, we didn't really have nothing to do." Brown slept in clothes he had worn for several days. He was unable to access other clothing at his grandmother's house because she was in the hospital.

Viron said between 7:00 and 8:00 a.m., "My sister asked him because I was being lazy at the time, my sister had asked him could he put my nephews in the car because my mother came to come get my nephews and my sister is pregnant now. So she couldn't carry them down the stairs, so he went and put them in the car." Brown left the apartment, then returned between 10:00 and 11:00, asking to use Viron's cell phone.

After the call, Brown said, "Me and Dorian's going to walk to the store, I'll be right back."

Viron then related the following sequence of events: "I still was laying down, but I wasn't asleep, I was on the phone with a lady friend of mine and we were just talking." Then, he heard a gunshot and went to the window. He saw Mike Brown's back and his hands raised in the air. Darren Wilson, wearing a black hat and glasses, stood directly in front of Brown. Wilson was "already out of his vehicle with a gun drawn . . . point blank range . . . four to five feet away . . . (the gun was pointing) towards the top of his skull . . . he is on his knees. . . . He was surrendering."

Viron swore that he observed Wilson fire a point blank shot into Brown's head: "I seen his body drop. And when I seen that, I ran outside. On my way downstairs, I heard several more shots. I didn't actually see them, but I heard them. . . . As soon as the bullet hit him, he dropped. . . . As soon as I hit the front door and got onto the balcony I heard, at least, I say about three to four shots. It was like a pause of me running down the steps, and then when I got to the end of the steps I heard several more shots. . . . When I ran out of the house, I ran over to the grass hill, people were out there crying and yelling. I was just like, they just kill my home boy for nothing, those were my exact words."

Kathi Alizadeh initiated the following interchange:

Alizadeh: And you admit today that a lot of what you told them (the police) on that day you didn't really see it?

Viron: Yes, it was more of me just finding out stuff here and there. . . . I don't think nobody would lie about something. So in my mind, I honestly believe that's what happened.

Alizadeh: You originally told the officers, or told the police that you saw the officer stand over Mike Brown after he fell in the street and stand over him and shoot him four more times.

Viron: Yes, that is what I was told, yes.

When asked if there was anything else he wanted to share with the grand jury, Viron said, "It's just about, not just, I've been dealing with, trust me, I've lived out in Ferguson for, I can honestly say about almost six years. Harassment, yes, I dealt through that growing up over there in that area. . . . I should be able to live, I should be able to feel safe where I live."

Alizadeh: Was Michael Brown ever with you when you were harassed by the police or do you know of any situations where he told you a story that he had been harassed?

Viron: Not him personally, but me, yes. Not with him, but we were harassed by—because Northwinds has and Canfield have security guards that legally got the right to hold guns and all that type of thing. Police-wise me and him together, no. If I was ever harassed, it was either by myself type of situation.

One of the more interesting interchanges came toward the end of Viron's testimony when Kathi Alizadeh asked, "What about why he wasn't living with his grandma? You said you knew."

Viron: That last little week, I don't know, they was just bickering and arguing a whole lot. And he got mad, I guess, they had an argument, he stormed out of the house and then he was at my house.

Alizadeh: Do you know what they argued about?

Viron: I don't because I was already at home, he just came and told me. She don't believe in me and I don't know what she said she was going to believe, I don't know if was the music thing we were doing. I honestly don't know but he was just like she don't believe in me or something.

It would be interesting to know the source of tension between Michael Brown and his grandmother. Somewhere along the line, he was introduced to Christian principles. The evening before he died, he discussed the role of God in helping him work through problems. The morning of his death, he met a white construction worker who was throwing a profane temper tantrum because of difficulty with his task. Brown stopped and said that the Lord Jesus Christ could help him with his anger. It seems plausible that his grandmother or grandmothers provided this Christian orientation.

On the other hand, Viron's influence was evident in the music he and "Big Mike" created. Their lyrics celebrated the NWA beliefs in misogyny, violence, and hostility toward police. Undoubtedly, Viron was the "Lil Vee" in Michael Brown's rap:

*You know we rock,*
*Lil Vee, I keep the Glock,*
*With 30 shots…*

Darren Wilson served as the foil when Michael Brown acted out:

*Shit talka, shit talka whatcha gonna do,*
*When a real killa, killa come for you…*

Viron stated that Michael Brown's grandmother disliked their music and did not believe in what the boys were doing. Although it is speculation on my part, common sense suggests her antipathy could have developed as she watched her grandson drawn into this antisocial persona. In any case, during fifteen minutes of bad choices that persona led to his death.

## GRAND JURY TESTIMONY OF WITNESS 18 GRAND JURY VOLUME X, OCTOBER 6, 2014, PP. 7 – 55.

Witness #18, a mature black female, and her husband, arrived at Canfield Green Apartments to visit her brother-in-law about 11:30 a.m. on August 9, 2014. As they came onto Canfield Drive, she saw Michael Brown and Dorian Johnson walking in the middle of the street. She reported, "And I said something to my husband in effect, why don't they just get on the sidewalk." She attributed their behavior "as them being kids not doing what they're supposed to be doing." She said that her husband "just kind of went around and did what we needed to do."

The couple parked their car then started up the apartment steps when she noticed a police car. She casually commented, "Oh, he's going to stop them and tell them to get on the sidewalk." By the time they reached the apartment landing, the police officer had stopped, apparently spoke to the boys, moved on briefly, and then, "He kind of whipped the car in reverse so it was at an angle." She then heard two gunshots while Wilson was still in his vehicle and the boys outside. After the second shot, she saw Michael Brown running away and Dorian Johnson "kind of disappeared."

Wilson got out of his vehicle and ran after Brown with both hands on his drawn gun. Brown reached a grassy area, stopped, looked at his right hand, and then "He turned back around and started going back towards the police officer." After the initial two shots, Wilson never fired his weapon until Brown turned around. Wilson stopped running when Brown turned, and they stood about 20 feet apart. As Brown came toward Wilson, the witness reported, "He just, I mean, he was walking back towards him and he started, he started shooting. He just kept shooting, he just kept shooting. And I asked my husband why is he, why won't that boy stop." She heard three or four shots, a pause, and then more shots. After the first string of shots, the witness said to her husband, "Maybe he doesn't have real bullets, maybe they are rubber bullets, he's not stopping, why doesn't he stop shooting." She asked her husband, "Why don't he just stop, why don't he just be still, why don't he just stop, and he didn't." As Brown approached Wilson, his palms faced forward, his arms were bent slightly at the elbows and by his side. His hands never rose above his head in a position of surrender.

When asked if it appeared necessary for the officer to shoot Brown the last volley of shots, she replied, "No . . . I just think it was too much. I mean, that's just me being a mother, this being a child, he was not charging at him, he did not have a weapon that I could see, I mean, I guess because these are the questions that I asked my husband."

Cathi Alizadeh followed up with more questions.

Alizadeh: And (Brown) started moving back towards the officers with his hands down like this, both you and (redacted) have both kind of said that there was a sense of frustration with you and why Michael Brown was still moving forward a little bit, sounds like you were both a little frustrated with that. Can you describe that a little?

Witness: I didn't understand why he just didn't stop and maybe get on his knees, just stop moving period. I just didn't understand why he kept going. I mean, I don't know if his parents have talked to him about ten and two and doing certain things when you are stopped. So, yes, I was frustrated.

I don't honestly think he had been taught what to do and that's just my personal opinion. Again, as I say, I have a -- son, and so you know, there is certain things that you do and don't do when you are approached by authority. And he just should have stopped. . . . I was frustrated because he just, I mean, he just should have stopped and I guess, I don't know, he should have did something different than just keep on moving.

Alizadeh: And you say he wasn't charging, he was just moving forward?

Witness: I want to say it is almost as if you tell someone to come here and they're coming, but he just kept walking, he just kept going, he just didn't stop. Even today, I don't know why, I don't understand that and when it was all going on I asked my husband why won't that child just stop.

The witness shared personal feelings about the environment in and around Canfield Green. She said, "This is why issues like this is why we don't frequent my (relatives). There is a lot of things going on down there and my son does not go down there unless he's with us."

This led to the following interchange with Shelia Whirley.

Whirley: Tell me what you meant by things are going on at Canfield apartments where you won't allow your son to go there without you?

Witness: It is just not an area that I want him in. I mean, it's just a lot of things that go on just, it's not a safe environment. . . . Just the complex in general. I just, it is not safe, it is not somewhere I want him. . . . Things happen, police are always down there. I don't know what goes on. I honestly don't go down there at night. So when I say I don't want my child there, he abide by what I tell him and he goes places where I feel he is going to be safe. . . . I don't want either one of my kids there. I'm going to tell you how I feel and my husband.

She described her son as a good kid; an excellent student with a 3.5 GPA who has never been suspended from school or in trouble.

Whirley then asked if she advised him to respect law officers.

Witness: Every time I tell him what to do and he even encountered being stopped by a police officer and it scared him to death because he was not doing anything, this is when he first learned how to drive. He was going to my aunt's house, it was dark and I don't know if you all are familiar with Parker Road, there are no lights on Parker, he had his high beams on. The police officer pulled him over and he stopped, he was not disrespectful, he was not belligerent, he pulled out his insurance, his license and police officer told him, young man, I'm just giving you a warning, turn your high beams off. And my child was so afraid, the officer wanted to know if he needed us to come and pick him up.

Note to Barack Obama—this black teenager was respectful and responsible. He is a good citizen. Although this was a police stop, the intent was to help a novice driver. The officer's automatic response was to be supportive when the boy was shaken by the stop. This is a practical example of what happens in the real world. Cooperation, initiative, and good citizenship pay dividends. It makes life easier for everyone. Color is irrelevant. On the other hand, this mother does not want to risk her son on streets of Ferguson where the thug mindset exerts its influence. It is dangerous. Good moms deplore it. Those who can avoid it.

## ANALYSIS AND COMMENTARY REGARDING EVENTS ON AUGUST 9, 2014

Autopsy results show that Michael Brown was high on marijuana at the time of his death. He was caught on videotape stealing from the Ferguson Market while manhandling and intimidating the clerk. Although the clerk told him he was going to call the police, Brown made no attempt to make himself inconspicuous. To the contrary, he kept the stolen cigarillos in his hand and walked down the middle of the street where no one could miss him because of his size and bright yellow socks with marijuana leaves on them.

When approached by Officer Wilson, the initial request was for Brown and Johnson to move out of the middle of the street and onto the sidewalk. If they complied, it is likely that Officer Wilson would have driven away without further scrutiny. Brown's defiant comment drew the officer's attention and gave him time to process the information regarding the description of the males who robbed the convenience store. With a second look through the rearview mirror, he noticed the cigarillos in Brown's hand and Johnson's black shirt.

Once Darren Wilson reversed his vehicle and blocked their path, Brown became aggressive. Wilson was blocked from exiting the SUV and witnesses reported seeing a "tussle." Depending on their viewing position, they described the Chevy Tahoe rocking side to side, Brown's feet shuffling or tapping outside the driver's side door, and arms pumping back and forth.

Dorian Johnson testified that Brown never had his hands or any part of his body in the vehicle. Furthermore, he claimed Wilson grabbed Brown with his left hand and tried to pull the 289-pounder into his vehicle, creating a tug of war. Like much of Johnson's testimony, this was incredible.

Forensic evidence supported Wilson's description of events. DNA analyses from the scene found Michael Brown's blood on the vehicle's interior door handle, Officer Wilson's gun and pants, and the exterior of the driver's-side front door. Brown's nasal mucus was on the exterior surface of the driver's-side back door.

Wilson's injuries supported his claim that Brown assaulted him. The physician's assistant testified that Wilson had scratches, bruising, a minor headache, and jaw pain. Wilson said his pain level was six on a scale from one to ten. She summarized that Wilson's injuries were superficial but consistent with impact injuries created by being punched and scratched.

When the first shot was fired inside the vehicle, the bullet went through the door panel indicating that the barrel of the weapon did not rise to the level of the window. This is consistent with Wilson's report that Brown struggled with him to gain control of the weapon and that Brown's grip prevented Wilson from raising the gun to a level where he had a clear shot. Brown backed off after the shot to see if he was wounded. Seeing no injury, he continued his assault.

The second shot fired from inside the vehicle hit Brown's thumb. This wound contained soot (coming from gun powder) and stippling (matter that becomes lodged in the skin when it is expelled from the gun along with the bullet). Soot typically indicates the shot was fired from a distance of less than nine inches. Its presence confirmed that Brown's hand was in close proximity to the gun when it went off. Furthermore, blood inside the Tahoe shows that his hand was in the vehicle when wounded.

There were no wounds on Brown's back, disproving Johnson's testimony that he was shot in the back while running away. Several credible black witnesses heard Darren Wilson command Brown to stop or get down. There is no credible evidence that Brown ever had his hands raised in a position of surrender. No credible witnesses heard him say "Don't shoot." Michael Brown was never on his knees. False claims in these areas generated a great deal of emotion, launching the "Hands up, don't shoot" fabrication. Looking back at his lyrics, the brutal truth is that Brown acted out his storyline with deadly consequences.

## AFTERMATH

The strongest reactions to Michael Brown's shooting came in two waves—those following his death and those in the wake of the grand jury finding no reason to press charges against Officer Darren Wilson. Protests were launched. "Die ins" were staged in cities across the country. The following premises underlie all these activities: America is a racist nation, blacks are oppressed, and whites and their police forces are the oppressors. The mainstream media lent credibility to these claims without ever challenging their veracity. This sort of journalism is the reason so many public opinion polls show the media is held in low esteem.

Following the grand jury verdict, Brown's stepfather, Louis Head, wearing his "I am Michael Brown" t-shirt, proclaimed, "If I get up there, I'm going to start a riot." He then stood on a car and repeatedly ranted for the crowd to "Burn this b*tch down!"[25] His antisocial appeal triggered massive damage to the community that included the destruction of twenty-five businesses, two police cruisers, and twelve civilian vehicles.

Al Sharpton was all over this situation, posturing and promoting racial divisiveness as much as possible. The overwhelming amount of national attention given to Ferguson was not enough for him. He claimed, "You thought you'd sweep it under the rug. You thought there'd be no limelight. We are going to keep the light on. . . .I'm sorry, I come out of the hood—the only way you make roaches run, you got to cut the light on." [26]

Threats of violence abounded. Protesters in Ferguson shouted, "What do we want? Darren Wilson! How do we want him? Dead!" In Philadelphia, fire department paramedic, Marcell Salters, posted an Instagram photo of two black men holding guns to the head of a white police officer. The caption read, "Our real enemy." This paramedic wrote he "never did or will like police. . . . Because of what I do I have to work with them but don't have to like them. . . . There are numerous crooked & corrupted cops (mostly white) & mostly they harass, beat, or kill innocents (mostly blks)." [27]

He went on, asserting, "need 2 stop pointing guns at each other & at the ones that's legally killing innocents." Salters took the image from a music video by rappers Uncle Murda and Maino called "Hands Up." The storyline for this rap is about someone pondering the events in Ferguson then arming himself to attack police. After reviewing Salters' comments and sentiments, Joseph Schulle, head of the firefighters union, said, "You get into a gray area when you start discussing First Amendment rights and responsibility as a city employee. I think that's what the department has to weigh in determining what type of punishment will be issued." [28]

If this picture showed whites holding guns to the head of a black official, Obama and his advisor, Al Sharpton, would be all over it. If a white public employee announced they never liked working with blacks, this would be the poster for racism and hate in America. Because this was black on white racism, it became a "First Amendment issue." It did not merit Obama's attention.

Nation of Islam leader Louis Farrakhan gave a November 21, 2014, speech at Morgan State, a predominantly black university in Baltimore. This was just days before the grand jury rendered their verdict regarding Darren Wilson. These statements were among his racially-charged comments: "We going to die anyway. Let's die for something. . . . Only violence can make white people listen to black people;" and, "We want some of this earth or we'll tear this goddamn country up." His comments were met with roaring applause according to Jim Hoft of *The Gateway Pundit.* [29] Farrakhan exclaimed, "The young—they are God's children and they are not going down being peaceful. Watch now, because once it starts, it's on. You may not want to fight, but you better get ready. Teach your baby how to throw the bottle if they can."[30] Days later, Ferguson was in flames. He recommends the same formula used in Detroit during the 1960s. How did that work out?

Such odious messages can find an audience. Three weeks after Farrakhan's university speech, Ismaaiyl Brinsley, an individual with mental health issues and a criminal history, shot his ex-girlfriend in the stomach then left Baltimore to fulfill a threat made on his Instagram account: "I'm Putting Wings On Pigs Today They take 1 Of Ours… Let's Take 2 of Theirs#ShootThePolice."[31] He drove to New York City where he assassinated Officers Rafael Ramos and Wenjian Liu who were on special patrol doing crime reduction work in the Bedford-Stuyvesant section of Brooklyn. An eyewitness told a *Daily Beast* reporter that "a lot of people were clapping and laughing" at the murder of the officers. Comments such as "they deserved it" and "serves them right" came from the crowd. [32]

**ANALYSIS AND COMMENTARY ON THE AFTERMATH.** With regard to Louis Head, what kind of person calls their neighborhood a "b*tch" and urges others to burn it down? This is antisocial evil and there is no excuse for it. Common sense says that he is morally and legally accountable for inciting such destruction.

Sharpton is a race hustler of the lowest denominator. And yet the media gives him a voice, including his own show on MSNBC. He tried to popularize his own chant through the "National Action Network" which was, "No justice, no peace." Sharpton defines "justice" in racially discriminatory terms with a disregard for facts. Blame and threat are his currency. Barack Obama brought him to the White House to server as an advisor.

Uncle Murda and Maino spew the same monotonous hate messages about niggas, guns, and killing. Such lyrics saturate the black community and wreak havoc. Marcell Salters, the Philadelphia Fire Department paramedic, would have been demonized and fired in a heartbeat if he were white and posted a picture of two white men with guns to the head of a black man.

For those of us who love America, Farrakhan's vitriol is sickening. Is any politician or member of the mainstream media willing to condemn his messages as antisocial and racist? Considering the timing and circumstances, he may have incited the murder of the two New York City police officers. If this is the case, there is blood on the hands of Morgan State University for allowing him to clamor for murder and anarchy.

From the beginning of the Ferguson affair, Barack Obama was unwilling to consider the word of a police officer. He jumped to the side of Michael Brown and his parents, who were "tit-for-tat" with Michael for a long time and didn't offer him a place to live during the attitude-shaping, dope-smoking, rap-writing days leading to his death. Obama painted police and prosecutors as unjust and our nation as racist with comments such as, "The frustrations that we've seen are not about a particular incident. They have deep roots in many communities of color who have a sense that our laws are not always being enforced uniformly or fairly."[33]

Charles Barkley was one of the few prominent black men to declare the Darren Wilson Grand Jury "got it right." He concluded, "The true story came out from the grand jury testimony. Three or four witnesses, who were black, said exactly what the cop said." With regard to the rioting, he declared, "There is no excuse for people to be out there burning down people's businesses, burning down police cars." He added, "They aren't black people, those are scumbags." He commented that "We, as black people, we have a lot of crooks. . . . We have to look at ourselves in the mirror. There is a reason that they racially profile us the way they do." Barkley urged the black community to stop seeing police as the enemy. He said, "We have to be really careful with the cops, because if it wasn't for the cops we would be living in the wild, wild west in our neighborhoods."[34]

It is important to get at crux of the matter. We need objectivity. We need a consistent standard for evaluating behavior and teaching children right from wrong, moral from immoral, and prosocial from antisocial. If we don't succeed in this task, towns like Ferguson will flounder, schools like Normandy High will fail, and America will suffer. America was built on common sense principles. Democracies only flourish when their citizens are respectful and responsible. Prosocial behavior yields happiness and prosperity. No good comes from defiance, hostility, and violence.

## CHAPTER 4

# A CLOSER LOOK AT DORIAN JOHNSON

D orian Johnson was the media darling of the Michael Brown case. No one loved him more than MSNBC. Three MSNBC interchanges with Johnson serve as examples of bias and slipshod journalism in the media. These are Al Sharpton's August 12, 2014, *PoliticsNation* interview of Dorian Johnson and his lawyer, Freeman Bosley,[1] Trymaine Lee's August 19, 2014, msnbc.com article,[2] and the November 25, 2014, edition of *All In with Chris Hayes*[3] featuring an interview with Johnson and lawyer James Wilson following the grand jury's decision not to indict Darren Wilson.

### AL SHARPTON AND DORIAN JOHNSON

Sharpton began his interview by saying, "The big question remains, what happened? We have two conflicting accounts, one from police and the other from eyewitnesses." He declared, with a hint of cynicism, "Here's the police version." St. Louis County Police Chief Jon Belmar gave the bare-bones summary, outlining the sequence of events as he understood them at the time. His statement was based on Darren Wilson's input and initial forensic evidence from the scene. He said an individual allegedly pushed the police officer back into the car, then physically assaulted him. There was a struggle over the officer's weapon. At least one shot was fired within the car. The officer exited the car and there was a shooting that produced fatal injuries.

Sharpton criticized Chief Belmar's summary because he "gave no detail about what happened outside the car where Brown was shot and killed nearly thirty-five feet away." This was the first indicator of Sharpton looking to get Whitey rather than looking for truth. He happily believed the thirty-five-foot estimate based on an early account offered by his star eyewitness, Dorian Johnson. Forensic evidence showed Michael Brown's body fell more than 159 feet from the police SUV; and, that was after he turned and came back toward Officer Wilson.

Crafting his language, Sharpton dramatized that "Dorian is still alive" and he has "a very different account of what happened." He then replayed the iconic video of Johnson talking to reporters on the day of the incident. For the purpose of this discussion, the following comments from Johnson are most salient:

*"And in the same moment the first shot went off and we looked down and he was shot and there was blood coming from him and we took off running. His weapon was drawn when he got out the car, he shot again and when my friend felt that shot he turned around and he put his hands in the air (Johnson raises his hands, palms facing forward and just above head level) but the officer still approached with his weapon drawn and he fired seven more shots."*

Johnson's description of events during Sharpton's August 12, program, three days after the on-scene interview, provided a different version that included these claims:

*"As we running, I step behind the first vehicle and stoop slightly. I could tell the officer was in shock because it took him at least two or three minutes before he initially got out the car after the first shot. It was almost like he had to make a judgment call and think about what he had just done or just saw. . . .*

*The officer is out the car now and I'm standing up now. And the officer is walking with his gun drawn but it's almost like he couldn't see me because I'm just standing right still in plain sight. . . .*

*As he got closer, he fired one more shot. That shot struck my friend in the back. He then stopped what he was doing and stopped to turn around with his hands in the air and started to tell the officer that he was unarmed and he was not. And before he could get his last words out the officer then fired several more shots and my friend went down in the fatal position and that's when I took off running."*

Al Sharpton never acknowledged or questioned the discrepancies between these two versions. Why? That would indicate that he was paying attention rather than making a concentrated effort to promote his anti-police/young black males are victims theme.

Autopsy results proved that Brown was never shot in the back. Another noteworthy element is Johnson's claim that he was "standing right in plain sight," obviously riveted on Michael Brown's final seconds that he previously described in lurid detail. Witness testimony refutes this assertion. In reality, Dorian Johnson hid behind a white 1999 Monte Carlo occupied by a female driver and male passenger after running from the police vehicle. The driver's testimony to the FBI is found in the *Grand Jury Transcript, Volume XII, October 13, 2014*, pp. 70–102.

This driver confirmed there was an altercation at Darren Wilson's vehicle. From her passenger-side view, she saw Wilson's Chevy Tahoe rocking from side to side and "a pair of feet just like tapping" on the ground next to the driver's door. At this point, she said the "guy with the dreads" (Johnson) had moved to the back of the vehicle looking "like he wanted to go, but he don't." The witness then heard gunshots and saw Michael Brown back up "like he was shocked." Brown ran past her car. A short time later, Wilson exited his vehicle and went past with his gun drawn. She described herself as "terrified" at this point and even "blacked out just a little bit."

By this time, Dorian Johnson was at the open passenger-side door of her car trying to get in. She said, "He was on the curb, but he had—he crawled. You could tell that he crawled. He was in the car and he just basically asked me could I get him away from here because it is crazy." She said, "I told him to get down. That's all I had, I mean, that was the only thing that come to my mind, just get down." They would not allow him in the car. He "disappeared" a short time later.

This testimony indicates that Johnson was not in a position to see Michael Brown and Darren Wilson as the final shots were fired. His claims about "Hands up," and "Don't shoot," and comments such as, "I could see it in his eyes. It was definitely like being shot like an animal" were inflammatory fabrications according to the credible testimony of this witness and others.

Toward the end of the interview, Sharpton turned to Johnson's attorney, former St. Louis Mayor Freeman Bosley Jr., and said, "Seems as though federal investigators are already seriously involved." Bosley reported that several witnesses met with the FBI, and Johnson would be scheduled for an interview. He then added the following statement:

> "One of the things that is just so disappointing about this is that we've got a situation in which this community here is insensitive to what happens to young African American males. What has occurred here with Big Mike is just another indication of what goes on around here. We got two other people that have been killed. We got a guy named Cary Ball who got shot twenty-seven times by the police. Officers actually stood over him, actually fired seven to ten shots into his body while he lays on the ground. We got another case involving a gentleman by the name of Antonio Johnson who was tased thirteen times

*by the police in two minutes in the city of Hazelwood. He died the next day.
This situation with Big Mike is just more of the same. We're so glad, Reverend
Sharpton, that you and the national media have decided to focus on the city
of St. Louis and what goes on here because this is critically important to us."*

Sharpton responded, "We're going to follow this story all the way through."

Bosley, Sharpton, Holder, and Obama all made the same clarion cry,
deploring the insensitivity and brutality of police officers and the victimization of
"communities of color." All four supported the report of "Hands up, don't shoot."
Obama used the bully pulpit to reinforce this message. He was totally willing to
jump to conclusions based on information from questionable sources, and to
make sweeping generalizations about the nature of the problem. As former mayor
of St. Louis, Bosley should have an idea of "what goes on around here." If he was
worth his salt, he would start with the following statistics:

The *2014 U.S. Census* indicated the population of St. Louis (City), Missouri,
was 317,419. The city's racial makeup was 46.6 percent white, 47.5 percent
black, 3.8 percent Hispanic, and 3.2% percent Asian. Saint Louis Missouri's
*UCR Homicide Analysis,* December 31, 2015, provided the following breakdown
of homicide victims and suspects:

| VICTIMS AND SUSPECTS BY RACE AND GENDER | | | | |
|---|---|---|---|---|
| **Victims** | **Male** | **Female** | **Suspects** | |
| Asian | 0 | 0 | Asian | 0 |
| Black | 148 | 25 | Black | 112 |
| Hispanic | 0 | 0 | Hispanic | 2 |
| Other | 0 | 0 | Other | 0 |
| White | 11 | 4 | White | 3 |

What does common sense tell us about these statistics? There is a tremendous
problem in the black community where too many blacks feel *Black Lives Don't
Matter.* Gangsta mentality rules the day. Problem solving begins with identifying
the problem. Ask the good people who live in St. Louis' troubled neighborhoods
and they will confirm the fact that black criminality detracts from the quality of
their lives and undermines their sense of security.

I have already discussed the Michael Brown case in detail. Brown robbed
a store, made himself extremely conspicuous after being told police would be

alerted, assaulted a police officer, and failed to stop his aggression when that choice was available. So, what about Cary Ball and Antonio Johnson?

Cary Ball was a twenty-five-year-old black male who crashed his car into parked vehicles after a high-speed chase on April 24, 2013.[4] He fled from police. During the pursuit, Ball pulled a .40 caliber Glock handgun from his waistband, pointed it at the officers, and ignored their command to drop his weapon. In response, one policeman fired twelve shots and the other sixteen shots, killing Ball. At the time of his death, he was a student at Forest Park Community College. The school's newspaper described him as an "emerging scholar" with a 3.86 grade point average. His criminal record showed he spent three years in prison for armed robbery when he was seventeen years old, then an additional two and a half years for probation violation.

Police Chief Sam Dotson requested a federal investigation of this case because several witnesses swore Ball threw his weapon down and tried to surrender before he was killed. U.S. Attorney Richard Callahan said the FBI investigation found no basis for criminal charges against the officers. In the end, "the number and extent of conflicting witness statements was well beyond what you normally encounter."[5] Credible witnesses who supported the police description of events were not willing to expose themselves through statements to the media.

His brother, Carlos, was asked why Cary would run from police in the first place. He responded that Cary was an ex-convict and knew it was against the law for him to carry a gun. But, "The way St. Louis streets work, we're afraid out here. We're afraid of the police. We're afraid of other youth who may want to pull a gun and fire on you. So, sometimes people have guns just to protect themselves, not with the intentions to do a criminal act with it." The *Uniform Crime Report Homicide Analysis* lends credence to his fear of "other youth." There is a major problem on the streets of St. Louis. It is disingenuous and counterproductive to say it starts with the police. Do the body count.

Antonio Johnson was a forty-year-old black male who was pulled over by police during July 2013 for suspicion of driving under the influence.[6] He allegedly drove southbound in the northbound lane of Charbonier Road in Hazelwood. The officer who stopped him called for backup when Johnson resisted arrest and became physical. Two other officers arrived and helped subdue Johnson. One officer suffered a bruised elbow and scrapes to his knees and arms.[7] Johnson died in the hospital after this altercation. In a wrongful death suit filed against the Hazelwood Police Force, the family's attorney, Freeman Bosley, charged the officers used excessive force.

Sadly, another Antonio Johnson died in St. Louis in March 2014. He was an eleven-year-old who was in a one-story bungalow with six other people when a gunman fired eight to ten shots through the window. Antonio was the only one hit. A bullet struck him in the head as he sat at his desk doing a spelling assignment that required him to spell thirteen words, then use each in a sentence. The first word on his list was "unsafe." Donna Horton, his fourth-grade teacher at Froebel Elementary School in St. Louis, described Antonio as a model student who took responsibility for his work and "gave 100 percent, whatever he did. Anyone would love to have him in their class." [8]

Reporter Joel Currier interviewed several members of the community following this murder. Tammy Harrington, 33, asked, "As parents, what are we supposed to say to our kids about all the crime that's going on?" Veronica Clark, 53, said, "It's really terrible that we can't even feel safe in our own homes." Deceal Burgess, 36, added, "Someone took the life of a young child, and it affects us all. When stuff like this happens, the reaction is for people to separate, not come together."[10] This is social oppression inflicted on the black community by black, antisocial *disrupters*.

If members of Black Lives Matter were true to their word, they would rally around the cause of eleven-year-old Antonio Johnson, a responsible student who was about to write a sentence using the word "unsafe" when he took a bullet to the head. They would create a *prosocial ripple effect* strong enough to establish an environment where Veronica Clark could feel safe in her home. They would work to reduce the St. Louis mayhem that saw 173 blacks murdered during 2015, almost exclusively at the hands of other blacks. This group has not shown the propensity to do the work necessary to make things better in black lives.

Use the *Prosocial Hierarchy* to consider the cases of Michael Brown, Cary Ball, and the older Antonio Johnson. Behavior has consequences. Oppositional behavior creates stress and tension. Defiant behavior leads to hostility and conflict. Violence places the individual's life in jeopardy and creates social havoc. All three of these black males made *bad choices*. These are not examples of police not knowing how to relate. These are tragic outcomes that result from breaking laws and becoming violent. Sharpton and Obama never acknowledge such realities. They collude in the White House to blame cops and defame America.

## TRYMAINE LEE AND DORIAN JOHNSON

A second MSNBC piece involving Dorian Johnson was the August 19, 2014, article written by national correspondent Trymaine Lee. Following Dorian Johnson's lead, Lee wrote that Michael Brown's final moments were "filled with shock, fear, and terror." He took Johnson at his word when he claimed to be just feet away from Brown, looking down the gun barrel pointed at his friend, and then seeing "fire come out of the barrel." Lee's article reported:

"I could see so vividly what was going on because I was so close,' said Johnson who said he was within arm's reach of both Brown and the officer when the first of several shots was fired at the teen. Johnson says he feared for his life as he watched the officer squeezing off shot after shot.

In reality, witnesses watched Johnson hop to the rear of the police cruiser looking like a scared rabbit during the altercation. Two shots were fired while Wilson was in his vehicle, with one of those shots hitting Michael Brown's thumb. It seems unlikely that Johnson could see either the emotion or the physical interaction between Brown and Wilson as the last strings of shots were fired because he was crawling to a car and pleading with the driver to get him "away from here because it is crazy."

Among others quoted in Lee's article was Brown family attorney, Benjamin Crump, a civil rights lawyer who previously represented the family of Trayvon Martin. Crump declared, "That baby was executed in broad daylight." The use of the term "baby" seems a bizarre characterization when referring to a six-foot-four-inch, 289- pound man who was high on marijuana, robbed a store, roughed up the clerk, assaulted a police officer, and was shot while posing an ongoing threat. "Executed" is another example of misguided, inflammatory rhetoric that makes its way onto MSNBC. Regardless of facts, headlines and sound bites are influential shapers of public opinion.

Lee quotes Brown's mother, Leslie McSpadden, who cried, "I just wish I could have been there to help my son." One has to wonder why Brown's best friend, Viron, said that Brown moved into an apartment with him, his pregnant sister, and her two children because "he (Michael Brown) didn't have nowhere else to go." Viron also testified, "From my understanding, him and his mother was always in tit for tat." (The meaning of tit for tat is "blow for blow in a retaliatory sense.") Viron related, "He (Brown) was bouncing back from houses to houses." It appears that Ms. McFadden was not there to help her son for some time.

Lee also wrote the following description of Darren Wilson's approach to the young men:

"About twenty minutes before the shooting, Johnson said he saw Brown walking down the street and decided to catch up with him. The two walked and talked. That's when Johnson says they saw the police car rolling up on them. The officer demanded that the two 'get the f—k on the sidewalk'."

This is lazy, sloppy journalism from Lee with no regard for facts. Johnson's grand jury testimony indicated that he and Michael Brown met at approximately 7:00 a.m. and were together until the time of Brown's death around noon. This was not a chance meeting and twenty-minute stroll. They were leaving the scene of a robbery, and Johnson admitted that he was in shock when Brown walked boldly down the middle of the street with stolen cigarillos spread out between his fingers, knowing that police had been alerted.

Finally, Lee reported that protests were being "stifled by rubber bullets and teargas fired at protesters by officers." There was no mention of the rioting, looting, and arson that did tremendous damage to the community of Ferguson. Is there any doubt why the general public has so little respect for the media?

## CHRIS HAYES AND DORIAN JOHNSON

The last MSNBC piece discussed here is the November 25, 2014, episode of *All In with Chris Hayes* that was aired after the grand jury recommended against indicting Darren Wilson. By November, there was enough written about Dorian Johnson's lack of reliability and credibility as a witness to steer clear of him. Chris Hayes obviously didn't care. MSNBC had an agenda. Hayes invited Johnson to reaffirm his false testimony. Hayes started by saying that Johnson "has given what can be described as heartbreaking testimony to the grand jury." Did Hayes read that testimony? Does "heartbreaking" capture the essence of what Johnson shared with the grand jury? That is not the descriptor I would use.

Hayes then asked questions intended to evoke responses that portrayed Darren Wilson as a villain and Michael Brown as a victim. These included: "And you say that Officer Wilson was the one who initiated contact by grabbing Mike Brown?" and, "Officer Wilson testified that he saw Mike Brown do a hop as if like an Olympian about to do a long jump. Did you see that?"

The description of Brown hopping like Olympic long jumper is markedly different from Wilson's grand jury testimony indicating Michael Brown did a little hop before "bulking up to run through the shots, like it was making him mad that I'm shooting at him." And his description of Brown leaning forward "like he was going to just tackle me, just go right through me." It is irresponsible for a reporter on national television to approach such an emotionally charged case without knowledge of readily available facts.

Lawyer James Wilson, who accompanied Johnson to this interview, provided this summation:

> *"It is important to note, and no one is saying this, Officer Wilson is shooting at them as they're running away from him and there has been no mention of this by Mr. McCollough when he gave his long soliloquy. He didn't mention that fact which certainly points to the fact that that level of force was not justified. Do you want to know what happened here and how this happened so quickly? It's because Darren Wilson came upon two young men who he didn't value as human beings. And that's how this happened so quickly."*

James Wilson joins the list of those disregarding forensic evidence and credible testimony while spinning a socio-political yarn. The crime scene investigation proved that no shots were fired at Michael Brown while he was running away. These two young men were approached because they were obstructing traffic flow while brazenly walking down the middle of the street, not because they were not valued as human beings. Contact with them was maintained because they matched the description of individuals who robbed a convenience store. The level of force was driven by Michael Brown's choice to become assaultive and pose a physical threat. These are the credible facts presented to the grand jury that led them to rule against indicting Darren Wilson.

At the end this segment, Hayes announced that a body was found that morning inside a car near where Michael Brown was killed and close to the site of Dorian Johnson's interview. The murder victim was twenty-year-old Deandre Joshua, a friend of Dorian Johnson. Deandre was shot in the head, doused with gasoline, and set on fire while seated in his Pontiac Grand Prix. The motive for his murder was unclear, although conspiracy theories postulated the involvement of a neighborhood "fixer" who believed Joshua provided testimony supporting Darren Wilson.

## DORIAN JOHNSON, THE LAW, AND THE TRUTH

Dorian Johnson has a history of problems with the law and a propensity to lie. He told the grand jury that he was arrested while attending Lincoln University in Jefferson City. He said he was with a group accused of stealing a package. A World Net Daily investigation by Gina Loudon found that Johnson was arrested on June 24, 2011, when he allegedly stole a package containing a backpack from in front of an apartment. He was caught on surveillance video abandoning the package at a nearby YMCA and apprehended by police.[11]

The grand jury assistant prosecutor asked Johnson about a false police report associated with this incident. He swore under oath, "I had both my school campus ID and my state ID in possession of me. When the officer asked me my name, I didn't say anything so much as just handed him my identification. I was mad at the time, again, I was a freshman in college, I'm kind of angry with the police, so I don't really want to say anything to them." The arrest record shows that Dorian repeatedly identified himself as Derrick Johnson and claimed to be sixteen years old (he was 19). He did not present his ID to the police; they found it hidden in his sock.

Johnson's trial was set for July 31st, but he failed to appear. He explained to the grand jury that, "When I got locked up, when I had got locked up, I got to the Jefferson City probation about the stealing, I guess I was in the middle of asking the judge can I do my probation in St. Louis because I was not from Jefferson City and in the middle of that we kind of lost contact, lost communication." Yeah, that makes sense. His lawyer, Freeman Bosley, insisted this case was "resolved." Barbara Schaffer, clerk for the Municipal Court of Jefferson City, confirmed there is a warrant for Johnson's arrest for the 2011 incident. The judge placed an order for Johnson's extradition if he was arrested within a fifty-mile radius of Jefferson City.

Dorian Johnson's latest contact with police came in May 2015. He was arrested for resisting or interfering with an arrest. Police were dispatched to the 5700 block of Acme Avenue in St. Louis when a caller reported a large group of people who were possibly armed. As an officer patted down a man with a bulge in his waistband thought to be a gun, Dorian's brother, Demonte Johnson, grabbed the police officer's arm to prevent the search. When the police detained Demonte, Dorian stood close to the officer, yelling in an attempt to stop the arrest of his brother. [12]

The *St. Louis Post-Dispatch* reported that Johnson and his lawyer, James Williams, filed a lawsuit against the city of Ferguson, Darren Wilson, and former police chief Thomas Jackson the week before this arrest. The suit claimed that Darren Wilson "acted with either deliberate indifference and/or reckless disregard toward Plaintiff's rights, targeting him without probable cause or any reasonable factual basis to support that Plaintiff had committed any crime or wrong, and using lethal force in an unjustified and unconstitutional manner." They described "an out-of-control Ferguson police department whose officers targeted African-Americans." The suit indicated Johnson was living in Metairie, Louisiana, a New Orleans suburb. [13]

Johnson shared revealing personal information during his grand jury testimony. He stated, "I knew he (Brown) wasn't someone like me, I knew he didn't grow up where I grew up from, where there was a bunch of violent gangs and violent stuff occurring all the time. I knew that much about because I read from his demeanor he didn't come up that way. I'm telling him about my life story and how I come up from a bunch of tragedies." Later in his testimony he reported, "Like I said, I've been shot at before, I've been shot once before, but I've been shot at in crazy situations, walking home from school and all."

Based on his self-description, Dorian operates in a dysfunctional social cauldron where he is in the middle of a "bunch of tragedies." His plunge from one whacky situation to another has nothing to do with police harassment. To understand his situation, it would be necessary to examine the folkways and mores dominant in his peer group and determine the principles guiding the behavior of him and his cohorts. Crazy seems to follow MSNBC's star eyewitness everywhere he goes, and truth seems to elude him.

Dorian Johnson is a prime example of how the mainstream media leads people astray with socio-political drama built on false premises. Inconsistencies in his testimony within the first few days should have alerted anyone paying attention that his input was unreliable. As early as August 19, 2014, Ben Shapiro of *Breitbart News* detailed how Johnson's "hands up" story was falling apart.[14] Despite this warning, the Washington Redskins brought politics into sport by running onto the field for an exhibition game with their hands up. Safety Branson Meriweather explained this was to "show our supporters what's going on in St. Louis." Hundreds of students at Howard University demonstrated with their hands up, and Harvard Law Professor Charles Ogletree called for Darren Wilson's arrest. This lawyer, teaching at the prestigious university founded by the Puritans, was more worried about a rush to judgment than due process. Nicole Tinson, a Yale Divinity School graduate student, claimed, "It's absolutely ridiculous. A man who holds his hands up is surrendering himself."[15]

Lucy McCalmont's article for *Politico* described Rep. Hakeem Jeffries' (D-NY) speech to the House of Representatives. He said, "Hands up, don't shoot. It's a rallying cry of people all across America who are fed up with police violence . . . in community, after community, after community . . . " He called for breaking "this cycle, this epidemic, this scourge of police violence all across America." He declared, "Now this is a problem that Congress can't run away from and the [Congressional Black Caucus] stands here today to make sure that Congress runs toward the problem"[16] And the political lemmings ran off the cliff of objectivity, knowledge, and reason.

Sarah Kinney Gaventa, associate rector at St. Paul's Episcopal Church in Ivy, Virginia, is the clear winner of the "Most Perverse 'Hands up' Story Award." *World Net Daily* presented excerpts from her August 2014 homily, which included the following pronouncements:

> *"He (Jesus) is a living God, who loved us so much and was so grieved by our inability to love him and one another, that he was willing to become human. He became Michael Brown. He became the victim of our sin, so we wouldn't have to sacrifice each other any more."*

> *"We don't know exactly what happened between Darren Wilson and Michael Brown; we have not yet heard the full story. But the shooting has tapped into underlying feelings of injustice about how black men are treated by police all over our country and those concerns are certainly backed by data."*

*"I think the problem of racism is so deeply ingrained in us that we aren't even aware of our bias. We shoot unarmed young black men, we suspend young black boys because deep down, we are afraid of them. Call it white privilege, call it systemic racism, whatever it is, we are infected."* [17]

"Jesus became Michael Brown?" Wow! To Ms. Gaventa, I recommend that she examine the crime statistics for St. Louis, or any American metropolitan area, to identify who is responsible for killing young black men. She should interview teachers at Normandy High School to gain insight regarding why black students are suspended. She should read Michael Brown's rap lyrics to determine if they should be incorporated into the *New Testament*. She should stop directing bigoted insults at white people. Finally, she should try getting facts and then judging people by the content of their character rather than the color of their skin.

## CHAPTER 5

# PRESIDENTIAL LEGACY: OBAMA THE COMMUNITY ORGANIZER

B
arack Obama declared during a 2008 presidential debate, "I can bring this country together. I have a track record, starting from the days I moved to Chicago as a community organizer." This stage of his career is important for understanding his mindset, motivation, and methodology. Examining this period of time provides insight about his actions and his legacy. As with the overview of America's character, I want to begin with a brief historical review—this time of socio-political movements of the 1960s.

Obama was born on August 4, 1961. The 1960s were rife with socio-political change. His mother, an anthropologist, served as an influential conduit for imprinting 60s personalities and principles into his value structure and belief system.[1] In his 1995 memoir, *Dreams from My Father: A Story of Race and Inheritance*, he described her as "a lonely witness for secular humanism, a soldier for New-Deal, Peace-Corps, position-paper liberalism." (Who talks about their mom like that?) In any case, what were some significant trends of the 60s?

### HISTORICAL CONTEXT: FIGURING OUT THE 60S

I entered the United States Army in September 1966 and was discharged in August 1969. My pay didn't exceed $121 per month during most of my first two years in the Army. My meager income and assignment to duty stations such as Augusta, Georgia, Sierra Vista, Arizona, and Killeen, Texas, assured that I was removed from mainstream culture. A year of combat in Vietnam took me further from the "real world."

While in the Army, I read news accounts of protests, anti-establishment demonstrations, and riots. Returning to a college campus a twelve days after leaving Vietnam and ten days after being discharged in Oakland, California, was culture shock. Things were different. It took time to grasp the new order. My discharge date was August 25, 1969, right on the heels of the August 15th– 18th Woodstock Festival. This musical rally of 400,000 underscored and accelerated changing attitudes toward drugs, sex, and rock and roll. Movies like 1969's *Easy Rider* represented a marked departure from 1966's best picture nominees—*A Man for All Seasons*, *Alfie*, and *Who's Afraid of Virginia Woolf?* Protests against the Vietnam War had intensified. College students conducted "sit ins," occupying the offices of university presidents who didn't have the gumption to throw them out. Black Panthers, Black Rage, and Black Power were in vogue. Riots caused substantial damage in cities including Washington, DC, Chicago, and Baltimore. None inflicted more economic and infrastructure damage than those in Detroit where July 1967 rioting saw 2,509 stores looted or burned, 388 families displaced, and 412 buildings burned or damaged to the point that they had to be demolished. Losses from arson and looting were estimated between $40 million and $80 million.[2] Detroit never recovered.

When I appeared bewildered by the cultural shift, a friend encouraged me to read Tom Wolfe. Wolfe was part of the New Journalism literary movement. He immersed himself in situations, serving as "an offstage narrator" looking for "truth" rather than "facts." Reading *The Electric Kool-Aid Acid Test* (1968) and *Radical Chic & Mau-Mauing the Flak Catchers* (1970) improved my understanding of the new order.

## THE ELECTRIC KOOL-AID ACID TEST.

This book tracked Ken Kesey and his Merry Pranksters as they participated in communal psychedelic "Acid Tests" in an effort to attain *transcendent states of intersubjectivity*. Kesey and his band traversed the country in their tripped-out school bus, interacting with the likes of the Grateful Dead, Hells Angels, and beat-generation guru Alan Ginsberg. The Prankster's drug-saturated trip between enlightenment and paranoia set the tone for the hippie and counterculture movements.

I saw more flaws than virtues in the hippie approach. Surrendering self-control to a drug that sent you careening into the surreal had no appeal for me. Hippie self-absorption and mental narcissism were turn-offs. The counterculture appeared vapid and devoid of substance. My skepticism seems corroborated by psychologist Martin Seligman who explored causes for the "epidemic" increase in depression spawned during this era. He offered the following summary:

> *"Our society has changed from an achieving society to a feel-good society. Up until the early 1960s, achievement was the most important goal to instill in*

*our children. This goal was then overtaken by the twin goals of happiness and high self-esteem. This fundamental change consists of two trends. One is toward more individual satisfaction and more individual freedom: consumerism, recreational drugs, daycare, psychotherapy, sexual satisfaction, grade inflation. The other is a slide away from individual investment in endeavors larger than the self: God, Nation, Family, and Duty."*[3]

This shift in focus toward "me" (Tom Wolfe wrote about the "Me Decade") and away from "we" undermines happiness at the personal level and erodes social cohesion. Witherspoon, Webster, and McGuffey were correct in believing that principles based on "we values" such as piety, patriotism, kindness, and charity are the ones most likely to provide a foundation for happy, meaningful lives.

How does this relate to Barack Obama? He admitted using marijuana and cocaine. In *Dreams From My Father*, he wrote: "I had learned not to care. I blew a few smoke rings, remember those years. Pot had helped, and booze; maybe a little blow (cocaine) when you could afford it." He also noted: "Junkie. Pothead. That's where I'd be headed: the final, fatal role of the young would-be black man. Except the highs hadn't been about that, me trying to prove what a down brother I was. Not by then anyway. I got just the opposite effect, something that could push questions of who I was out of my mind, something that could flatten out the landscape of my heart, blur the edges of my memory." Spoken like a true proponent of *transcendent states of intersubjectivity*. Psychologically, it would be interesting to analyze the role that being a "would-be black man" and "down brother" play in his personality and politics.

David Maraniss, author of the biography *Barak Obama: The Story*, indicated that while a student at Punahou School, Obama traveled with a group calling themselves the Choom Gang. They rode around in a VW van and hung out on Mount Tantalus on Oahu. He reported, "They parked single file on the grassy edge, turned up their stereos playing Aerosmith, Blue Oyster Cult, and Stevie Wonder, lit up some 'sweet-sticky Hawaiian buds,' and washed it down with 'green bottled beer'." Obama claimed this helped him deal with the pressures of Punahou where he was a student from fifth grade through graduation in 1979.[4]

To understand Obama, it is worth looking at Punahou. Their website indicates they are a kindergarten through twelfth grade college preparatory school with an enrollment of 3,768 students. Their 2015–2016 tuition was $22,050. Ninety-three percent of students carry grade-point averages of 3.0 or higher. Class of 2015 SAT scores showed that 93 percent earned 500 or better on Critical Reading, 98 percent earned 500 or higher on Math, and 92 percent earned 500 or higher on Writing.[5] Taken as a whole, the Choom Gang sounds like a group of elite preppies. Punahou is the antithesis of places like Normandy High School. If we are to talk about those who are privileged, we could consider Obama's Panhou-Occidental-Columbia-Harvard education while receiving substantial financial assistance along the way. It is a disgrace that gratitude for America's right-to-rise principle never enters his prime-time message.

## RADICAL CHIC

Wolfe's book, *Radical Chic and Mau-Mauing the Flak Catchers*, is comprised of two essays. The underlying dynamic shared by these pieces is the intersection of *white guilt* and *black rage*. "Radical Chic" was a term coined to describe the commitment of wealthy (especially Jewish) liberals to support social radicals. The essay describes a fund-raiser hosted by conductor Leonard Bernstein and his wife in their thirteen-room penthouse at 895 Park Avenue to raise money for the violent, anti-white Black Panther Party. Oakland Field Marshal Donald Cox was guest of honor. Attendees included Otto Preminger and Barbara Walters. The house staff consisted of three white South American servants, plus Lenny's white chauffeur and dresser. The Bernstein's were known to help friends attain white South American servants. These friends referred to the Bernsteins, "good-naturedly and gratefully, as 'the Spic and Span Employment Agency.'"[6]

The Black Panthers were chosen as recipients of this group's attention and money because Bernstein and friends viewed civil rights organizations such as the NAACP as too mainstream. They were drawn to the Black Panthers' militant posture. The heart of this group's political stance was outlined in *The Black Panther Party for Self-Defense Ten-Point Platform and Program*. This document was drafted in 1966 by Huey Newton and Bobby Seale who gave it the grandiose description of being a "combination of a Bill of Rights and a Declaration of Independence." This document includes the following declarations:

### What We Want Now!
1. We want freedom. We want power to determine the destiny of our Black Community.
2. We want full employment for our people.
3. We want an end to the robbery by the white men of our Black Community. (Later changed to "we want an end to the robbery by the capitalists of our black and oppressed communities.")
4. We want decent housing, fit for shelter of human beings.
5. We want education for our people that exposes the true nature of this decadent American society. We want education that teaches us our true history and our role in the present day society.

6. We want all Black men to be exempt from military service.

7. We want an immediate end to POLICE BRUTALITY and MURDER of Black people.

8. We want freedom for all Black men held in federal, state, county and city prisons and jails.

9. We want all Black people when brought to trial to be tried in court by a jury of their peer group or people from their Black Communities, as defined by the Constitution of the United States.

10. We want land, bread, housing, education, clothing, justice and peace.[7]

In summary, this group wanted guaranteed employment, housing, education that allows them to defame those funding this education as oppressors, racially-based exemption from military service in time of war, release of all black prisoners regardless of how heinous their crimes, and free land, bread, housing, education, clothing, justice, and peace. Barbara Walters attended the party. Leonard Bernstein assembled ninety friends to fund the cause. Lyndon B. Johnson altered the course of our nation to accommodate their demands. Thomas Jefferson, John Adams, and the founding fathers rolled over in their graves. John Witherspoon deemed this to be *perfect nonsense.*

Results of the educator survey presented earlier in this book yielded what I believe are common sense notions of good citizenship: (1) respect and responsibility; (2) motivation, self-control, and compliance; and, (3) parental involvement and supervision. There is nothing in the Black Panther Ten Points that shows understanding of or commitment to good citizenship. There is no sign of personal or group responsibility. If the ten "we wants" were written in a constructive form such as, "We dedicate ourselves to working for . . . " the black community could be better off. This amended document would promote responsibility and discourage the destructive "gimmie" cycle of welfare dependence.

## The Black Panther Ten-Point Platform continued with examples of "What we believe:"

- The federal government is responsible and obligated to give every man employment or a guaranteed income.

- The American racist has taken part in the slaughter of over 50,000,000 black people.

- Housing and land should be made into cooperatives so that our community, with government aid, can build and make a decent housing for its people.

- Black people should not be forced to fight in the military service to defend a racist government that does not protect us. . . . Black people are being victimized by the white racist government of America.

During Black Panther Donald Cox's presentation to Bernstein and friends, Otto Preminger challenged his statement that America is the most repressive country in the world by asking, "Do you mean dat zis government is more repressive zan de government of Nigeria?" Cox answered, "I don't know anything about the government of Nigeria."[8] Tellingly, Preminger later apologized for being rude and ponied up $1,000 for the cause.

The Black Panthers wanted to rewrite the history of blacks in America. This would be an interesting read in view of the fact their representative appeared to know nothing about Africa. Lack of knowledge lends itself to fiction rather than fact. Claiming that 50,000,000 blacks were slaughtered in racist America is fiction. Relying upon the *Trans-Atlantic Slave Trade Database*, Dr. Henry Louis Gates, Jr., Director of the Hutchins Center for African & African American Research at Harvard University, reported that between 1525 and 1866 12.5 million Africans were shipped to the New World. Approximately 10.7 million survived the trans-Atlantic voyage. The majority of slaves went to the Caribbean and South America, with Brazil receiving 4.86 million. Three hundred and eighty-eight thousand were shipped directly to North America. An estimated 60,000 to 70,000 Africans entered through the Caribbean, bringing the total to approximately 450,000. Sixteen percent of slaves in the United States came from eastern Nigeria (a place unknown to Donald Cox). Twenty-four percent came from the Congo and Angola. The bulk of slaves arrived before the United States was a nation.[9]

In an April 23, 2010, op-ed piece for the *New York Times*, Gates explained that 90 percent of slaves shipped to the New World were captured by Africans and then sold to European traders. This runs counter to Alex Haley's depiction of Kunta Kinte being snared by evil whites in the mini-series *Roots*. Gates cited Frederick Douglass' comment:

> *"The savage chiefs of the western coasts of Africa, who for ages have been accustomed to selling their captives into bondage and pocketing the ready cash for them, will not more readily accept our moral and economical ideas than the slave traders of Maryland and Virginia. . . . We are, therefore, less inclined to go to Africa to work against the slave trade than to stay here to work against it."[10]*

Gates noted that the slave trade was significantly reduced by 1807 (nineteen years after ratification of our Constitution) because of the strong work of abolitionists, with Yale and the Teachers College of Cincinnati being two of the most influential centers leading this effort.

In less than a century after earning its independence as a nation, the United States of America abolished slavery. The Black Panthers plant the emotional fiction that America is a racist nation that slaughtered 50,000,000 blacks in the minds of the uninformed. Bernie Sanders proclaims we are a nation founded on racist principles. Both of these assertions are erroneous, harmful fictions.

During an April 2016 speech at Tindley Temple United Methodist Church in Philadelphia, Sanders said that he would apologize for America's history of slavery if he is elected president:

*"There's nothing that anybody can do to undo the deaths and misery—how many people we don't even know who died on the way over here from Africa in the ships. But we have got to do everything we can to wipe the slate clean by acknowledging the truth. You know truth is not always an easy thing. There are a lot of things that we have done in this country that are shameful. We have got to recognize that and own up to it."*

He went on to add the following statement:

*"There is legislation introduced by some members of the Black Caucus, which I support, which takes a look at those communities around America which have long-term structural poverty issues and they become the communities that receive the highest priority for federal funding. In other words, let us make sure that in every way, federal funding goes to those communities who need it the most, and in most cases that will be minority communities."*[11]

From these pronouncements, it is obvious that Sanders is a progressive believer in the following: (a) redistributing wealth; (b) declaring America a racist nation; and, (c) allowing the Congressional Black Caucus direct where money will be allocated. Lyndon B. Johnson launched a trillion-dollar program in the 1960s that sounded remarkably the same. How did that work out? Why are so many black communities in worse shape today than they were then? Why is "the hood" so difficult to survive in and escape from?

Money does not solve social problems. Good citizenship does. Think back to Normandy High School and its "culture of violence," where as many as five fights erupt in hallways and classrooms each day, where a teacher gets pepper-sprayed by a student while trying to break up a fight., where teachers relate that, "Teaching is very difficult. Teachers get cussed out, yelled at. There are so many write-ups you can't keep up," where police and fire crews are called eighty-three times because students set toilet paper, soap dispensers, old papers, and books on fire.

Within a week of Sanders' Philadelphia speech, the *Philadelphia Inquirer* published an article titled, "Phila. School District Still Struggling to Fill Teacher Vacancies." This article stated that "with little more than two months remaining in the academic year, more than 100 (the actual number was 139) teacher vacancies remain across the Philadelphia School District, resulting in thousands of students being taught by uncertified teachers." [12] This unfortunate circumstance creates chaos, denigrates instructional quality, and generates unnecessary costs. The school district said they would offer a variety of "summer enrichment programs" to help students who did not have a regular teacher for more than one-third of the school year. Not have a regular teacher for more than one third of the school year? This is incredible but understandable when the percentage of severe student disruptors reaches a level where effective teaching becomes impossible and teachers are psychologically and physically battered. This is bail out or burn out. Spokesman Fernando Gallard said the district is perpetually understaffed because "a strong job market has given teaching candidates more options while making it harder for the district to fill classrooms."[13]

I know the school districts around Philadelphia. Some suburban schools have more than 139 applicants for a single teaching position—that's a fact. There is no teacher shortage in the area. The critical factor is school climate. This is not a black/white or rich/poor issue. It hinges on whether *prosocial* or *antisocial* behavior dominates the setting. Productive suburban schools are not some mystical product of white privilege. They thrive because of good citizenship that is colorblind. Money can't buy it. It requires the correct principles.

## MAU-MAUING THE FLAK CATCHERS

This essay described Wolfe's observation of the Office of Economic Opportunity in San Francisco that administered anti-poverty programs. Foley explained that Wolfe "uses the term 'mau-mauing' to describe the activity of threatening the bureaucrats and white leadership in order to secure patronage."[14] Wolfe described "mau-mauing" in the following way:

*"Ninety-nine percent of the time whites were in no physical danger whatsoever during mau-mauing. The brothers understood through and through that it was a tactic, a procedure, a game. If you actually hurt or endangered somebody at one of these sessions, you were only cutting yourself off from whatever was being handed out, the jobs, the money, the influence. The idea was to terrify but don't touch. The term mau-mauing itself expressed*

*this game-like quality. It expressed the put-on side of it. In public you used the same term the whites used, namely, "confrontation." The term mau-mauing was a source of amusement in private."*

The term *mau-mauing* said, 'The white man has a voodoo fear of us, because deep down he still thinks we're savages. Right? So we're going to do that Savage number for him.' It was like a practical joke at the expense of the white man's superstitiousness."[15]

## Wolfe described how gangs hustled the system:
"Some of the main heroes in the ghetto, on a par with the [Black] Panthers even, were the Blackstone Rangers in Chicago. The Rangers were so bad, the Rangers so terrified the whole youth welfare poverty establishment, that in one year, 1968, they got a $937,000 grant from the Office of Economic Opportunity in Washington. The Ranger leaders became job counselors in the manpower training project, even though most of them never had a job before and weren't about to be looking for one. . . . In San Francisco the champions were the Mission Rebels. The Rebels got every kind of grant you could think of, from the government, the foundations, the churches, individual sugar daddies, from everywhere, plus a headquarters building and poverty jobs all over the place.

The police would argue that in giving all that money to gangs like the Blackstone Rangers the poverty bureaucrats were financing criminal elements and helping to destroy the community. The poverty bureaucrats would argue that they were doing just the opposite. They were bringing the gangs into the system.

## OBAMA THE COMMUNITY ORGANIZER
This brings us back to Barack Obama, community organizer in the city of Chicago. Byron York wrote an excellent overview describing this stage of Obama's career in the *National Review* while the 2008 presidential campaign was in full swing.[16] York noted that in *Dreams From My Father*, Obama talked about defining the objectives of a community organizer to college classmates by saying, "I'd pronounce on the need for change. Change in the White House, where Reagan and his minions were carrying on their dirty deeds. Change in the Congress, compliant and corrupt. Change in the mood of the country, manic and self-absorbed. Change won't come from the top, I would say. Change will come from a mobilized grass roots."[17]

Several aspects of his explanation are notable. First, is the air of condescension. He doesn't explain, he "pronounces." His negativity about a sitting president and congress is standard political fare. He renders a contemptuous assessment of

Americans as manic and self-absorbed, a descriptor that does not fit most of the Americans I know. His reference to change is geared toward denouncing existing institutions rather than identifying and solving problems. Finally, he wants to mobilize the "grass roots." In Chicago, and all the way through his stay in the White House, his grass roots focus seems locked on "communities of color," which translates to blacks with a passing nod to Hispanics.

Obama worked as a community organizer in Chicago for three years, 1985 to 1988. He explained in his memoir that he went to Chicago to "organize black folks."

Jerry Kellman, the man who hired Obama, explained to Byron York, "Barack had been very inspired by the civil-rights movement. I felt that he wanted to work in the civil-rights movement, but he was ten years too late, and this was the closest he could find to it at the time." His ultra-liberal anthropologist mother imprinted sentiments of the 1960s in his heart and mind.

## THE CHICAGO INFLUENCES

Chicago has a well-established history of activism. The Abbie Hoffman-led Chicago Seven, joined by Bobby Seale to form the Chicago Eight, were notorious for their rallies, marches, and demonstrations, including disruption of the 1968 Democratic National Convention. Another Chicago activist, considered the founding father of community organizing and an influence for Obama, was Saul Alinsky (1909–1972). Alinsky's efforts began in the Chicago stockyards during the 1930s. He detailed his "organizing" strategies in *Rules for Radicals* (1971), a book published shortly before his death. York summarized Alinsky's essentials for becoming a successful organizer: (a) be "an abrasive agent to rub raw the resentments of the people of the community; fan latent hostilities of many of the people of the community;" (b) get the hostilities "whipped up to a fighting pitch;" then, (c) steer the group toward confrontation through picketing, demonstrating, and hell-raising. Alinsky dedicated his book to "the first rebel"—Lucifer.[18] Ah, the Old Deluder. This book is the *How-to Manual for Mau-mauing.*

Serge Kovaleski pointed out in the *New York Times* that Obama spent one third of his memoir's 442 pages describing his community organizing days in Chicago. Obama referred to this period as "the best education I ever had, better than anything I got at Harvard Law School." Once in the community organizer role, he set out to find a cause. He began by conducting one-on-one interviews with residents on the South Side and then worked to build a network of alliances through church contacts, starting with the Developing Communities Project, a program initiated by white Catholic priests. In order to gain credibility with black church leadership, he was pressed to join a congregation. He chose Trinity United Church of Christ on 95th Street because he was attracted to the message of the church's leader, Rev. Jeremiah Wright. [19]

Wright came from a mixed-race (white father, black mother), middle-class family residing in the Germantown section of Philadelphia. Charles Johnson provided an overview of the relationship between Obama and Wright, as well as describing Wright's "race-based theology" in the January 2012 issue of *The American Spectator*:

- Obama was an active member of this congregation for twenty years.

- Obama said that Wright was "like family to me. [He] strengthened my faith, officiated my wedding, and baptized my children."

- The writing of James Cone, author of *Theology and Black Power,* strongly influenced Wright. According to Johnson, "Cone taught that Christianity needed to be freed from 'whiteness.' He and Wright conceived of a Christianity in which black rage and the black power ideology fused with Marxist thought. According to Cone, 'black people must find ways of affirming black dignity which do not include relating to whites on white terms.' Integration was impossible because it was brought about by 'black naivete' and 'white guilt.'"

- Wright was loyal to Malcolm X and Louis Farrakhan.

- Wright routinely cited conspiracy theorists who believe Jewish doctors working for the United States government created HIV/AIDS.

- In [Wright's] church-associated Kwame Nkrumah Academy, the congregation's children were taught that "[h]istorically, Europeans tried to build themselves up by tearing down all that Africans had done."

- In a sermon marking the tenth anniversary of 9/11, Wright invoked Malcolm X's statement made after JFK's assassination: "America's chickens! Coming home! To roost!" This message suggested that white America was getting its just deserts.[20]

## OBAMA'S ACCOMPLISHMENTS IN THE COMMUNITY

In three year's time, the list of Obama's accomplishments within the community was meager. Those who worked closely with him felt that his most lasting accomplishment was strengthening the Developing Communities Project. This is a grant-getting institution that works on projects such as after-school programs, drug prevention, and voter registration. The bulk of its money (75 percent) comes from government grants, with the rest donated by liberal foundations.

Obama's community organizing produced two victories. One was getting the Chicago Housing Authority to remove asbestos from Atgeld Gardens, a low-rise housing project built in the 1940s. The second was forcing the Mayor's Office of Employment and Training to open a summer-jobs program south of 95th Street. *The New York Times* commented, "It is clear that the benefit of those years to Mr. Obama dwarfs what he accomplished."[21]

## Byron York offered the following summary:

*"But Obama's time in Chicago also revealed the conventionality of his approach to the underlying problems of the South Side. Is the area crippled by a culture of dysfunction? Demand summer jobs. Push for an after-school program. Convince the city to spend more on this or that. It was the same old stuff; Obama could think outside the box on ways to organize people, but not on what he was organizing them for."* [22]

It is important to examine how words relate to actions. Obama came to Chicago in order to "organize black folks." That is significantly different from coming to "solve problems experienced by black folks." His projects were minor initiatives demanding something from the system. His lasting contribution was strengthening a nonprofit group that would continue asking for things from the system. Yvonne Lloyd, a census taker on the South Side, supported York's description of South Side's dysfunctional system. She said, "When you look at those forms from the census, you had three or four generations in one apartment—the grandmother, the mother, the daughter, and then her baby. It (welfare) was supposed to be a stepping stone, but you've got people that are never going to leave." York observed, "When a real attempt to break through that culture of dysfunction— the landmark 1996 welfare-reform bill, now widely accepted as one of the most successful domestic-policy initiatives in a generation—came up, Obama vowed to use all the resources at his disposal to undo it: 'I made sure our new welfare system didn't punish people by kicking them off the rolls.'[23]

Use common sense to examine priorities that would improve the quality of life in Chicago's black communities. Anyone coming to city with the goal of solving problems that impact these neighborhoods would know within two days of reading newspapers and talking to the man in the street that crime and education should be the first priorities. We'll skip the struggles in Chicago's educational system, because I have already reviewed the challenges faced in urban schools.

What do headlines tell us about crime in Chicago? The January 2, 2016, edition of the *Chicago Tribune* addressed the issues of violence and homicides in Chicago. Most of Chicago's violent crime takes place in the predominantly black South and West Sides. The city reported the following death toll: [24]

| Chicago Homicides by Year | |
|---|---|
| 2011 | 437 |
| 2012 | 506 |
| 2013 | 420 |
| 2014 | 416 |
| 2015 | 468 |
| Five-year Total | 2,247 |

This level of carnage in the city that Obama calls his own is horrible. One would hope problems of this magnitude didn't exist while the he was "organizing black folks." Oops. Here is the reality check regarding Chicago's homicide rates during those years:

| Chicago Homicides by Year[25] | |
|---|---|
| 1985 | 666 |
| 1986 | 744 |
| 1987 | 691 |
| 1988 | 660 |
| Four-year Total | 2,761 |

During a February 2008 candidate debate, Obama said, "I can bring this country together. I have a track record, starting from the day I moved to Chicago as a community organizer." His track record shows that during his organizing years there were 2,761 murders in Chicago, with the vast majority of victims being black. He invested his time and energy on having the city remove asbestos from a housing project on the South Side while thousands died in the streets. There was no commitment to saving black lives. There was no hint that he wanted to identify Chicago's greatest problems let alone go to work trying to solve them.

Obama's former Chief of Staff and Chicago Mayor, Rahm Emanuel, recently inferred that Obama's presidential vilification of police officers was contributing to an increase in Chicago's violence, with a 13 percent increase in both homicides and violent crime between 2014 and 2015. The October 13, 2015, edition of the *Chicago Tribune*, quotes Emanuel:

> *"What happened post-Baltimore, what happened post-Ferguson is having an impact."* He commented, *"Officers themselves are telling me about how the news over the last fifteen months impacted their instincts: Do they stop or do they keep driving?"* Police ask themselves, *"When I stop here, is it going to be my career on the line? And that's an honest conversation. And all of us who want officers to be proactive, to be able to do community policing in a proactive way, have to encourage them, so it's not their job on the line or that judgment call all the time that if they stop, this could be a career-ender."*[26]

And, the beat goes on. The March 28, 2016, *New York Times* reported, "As of Friday, 131 people had been killed here (in Chicago) in the first months of 2016, an 84 percent rise in homicides from the same period in 2015. There had been 605 shootings, nearly twice as many as at this point last year." Daysha Wright, a twenty-one-year-old nursing student and mother of a two-year-old was shot to death while sitting in a car. Gloria Johnson, thirty-seven, who works in a restaurant in Austin, a particularly violent part of the city, said, "I'm really tired of it, and tired of worrying." Reverend Ira Acree lamented, "Unless something radical takes place, it's going to be a blood bath this summer."[27] He wanted to call in the National Guard. South Side resident April Lawson had a novel idea. She recommended a "sex strike," with abstinence until the men of Chicago put down their guns. She reasoned, "You have to hit people where it hurts."[28]

The April 21, 2016, *Chicago Tribune* continued documenting the death toll. It noted that Chicago passed the 1,000 shooting-victim mark six to nine weeks ahead of the pace set during the four previous years. The 1,000th victim was a sixteen-year-old boy who was shot at the Atgeld Gardens public housing complex, the place Obama saved from asbestos. The homicide total reached 161, 64 percent higher than the 98 killed during the same interval in 2015. Although New York City and Los Angeles both exceed Chicago in population, their combined total of people shot, 246 and 328, respectively, was lower than that of Chicago.[29]

Here is the *Catch 22* conundrum imposed on police throughout the Barack Obama presidential era. When police approach blacks with stop-and-frisk or other preventative tactics, they are *racial profiling*. If they drive past suspicious characters or activities because they do not want to be accused of profiling, they are not *proactive* enough. Obama never places responsibility on the community. It's always about the police. This myopic, racist posture has deadly results. He was given eight years to provide answers, but he never asked the right questions. It was predictable. Look at his track record as a community organizer in Chicago.

The cost of this violence is tremendous. According to the *Chicago Tribune*, the city has paid more than $100 million dollars in police overtime between 2013 and 2016 to provide additional services in dangerous neighborhoods. But, interim Police Superintendent John Escalante reported that "social media taunting, social media threats, social media disrespecting has really increased over the last couple years." Police have taken to calling this "cyberbanging." Spurred on by NWA's "somebody f*ck with me, I'm gonna f*ck with them" mantra, the carnage is never-ending. As a result, the stories keep coming.

Nine-year-old fourth-grader Tyshawn Lee was lured from playing basketball into a South Side alley where he was fatally shot in the head execution style. A short time later, his father was accused of shooting three people.[30]

The fiscal liability of this violence is staggering. Analysis of government statistics by the Pacific Institute for Research and Evaluation showed the following costs of gunshot wounds and deaths to the government in 2010:

- $5.4 billion in tax revenue lost because of lost work

- $4.7 billion in court costs

- $1.4 billion in Medicare and Medicaid costs for firearm injuries and deaths

- $180 million in mental health care costs for gunshot victims

- $224 million in insurance claims processing

- $133 million for responding to shooting injuries

Dr. Manish Sethi, a trauma surgeon at Vanderbilt University in Nashville, Tennessee, was a researcher for this study. He participated because "a bunch of African-American kids with gunshot wounds" continually entered his emergency room. He found that 79 percent of victims were on Medicaid, and three out of four were Black.[31]

If we look for root causes, we have to consider the welfare state launched by LBJ's Great Society. The problem of welfare dependency, family dysfunction, and fatherless homes, compounded by rap homilies that teach children antisocial lessons, is a recipe for disaster at every level. Children, families, communities, and the nation all pay the price.

Let's go full circle. Ethical/moral principles have at least four related purposes:

1. To keep society from falling apart
2. To ameliorate human suffering
3. To promote human flourishing
4. To resolve conflicts of interest in just ways

Thomas Reid said, "...before men can reason together, they must agree in first principles; and it is impossible to reason with a man who has no principles in common with you." Improvements on the South Side of Chicago will not come from the Obama's Department of Justice or Illinois' ACLU putting more responsibility and blame on police. We have to look at the community. Obama never hinted at such an analysis. We need shared principles of right and wrong. Money is not and never will be the answer. Shared moral principles are and always will be.

## CHAPTER 6

# CASE STUDY: HENRY LOUIS GATES, JR.

The 2009 case of Professor Henry Louis Gates of Harvard University and Sergeant James Crowley of the Cambridge Police Department was the first significant racial controversy confronting Barack Obama after his inauguration as the nations' first black President. Obama's uninvited and uninformed injection of himself into this situation revealed his racial bias and served as a harbinger for what the following seven years would bring.

## HENRY LOUIS GATES

Gates, the aforementioned Director of the Hutchins Center for African & African American Research at Harvard University, is living proof of America's primary principle—*the right to rise*. He was born on September 16, 1950, in Keyser, West Virginia. His father worked in a paper mill and moonlighted as a janitor. His mother was a house cleaner. Gates graduated from Piedmont High School in 1968, attended Potomac State College, then went on to earn a BA in history from Yale University. He received an Andrew W. Mellon Foundation Fellowship that allowed him to attain a PhD in English literature from Cambridge University in England. He joined Yale University's Afro-American Studies Department in 1975, then moved to Cornell and Duke Universities before being recruited by Harvard in 1991.[1]

Common sense indicates that Gates should express gratitude for America as the land of opportunity where individuals are encouraged to use education to rise from humble beginnings to fame and fortune, regardless of race. In an era of affirmative action and racial preferences, it seems likely that skin color worked in his favor for opening doors and gaining support along the way. His fellowship stemmed from the social conscience and generosity of Andrew Mellon (1855–1937), a Scotch-Irish banker, businessman, and philanthropist whose values were influenced by *McGuffey's Readers*.

On June 16, 2009, Sergeant James Crowley of the Cambridge Police Department arrested Gates for disorderly conduct. This event made national news. The word "bias" has many implications:: prejudice, partiality, unfairness, preconceived notion, forgone conclusion, and distortion of results. President Obama felt the need to use his bully pulpit to focus the national spotlight on this local event, launching his presidential platform that propagates his bias that white police officers target, abuse, and incarcerate black men, primarily because of the color of their skin.

During a prime time news conference intended to deal with the topic of health care, the final question referred to the Gates case. Obama replied:

> My understanding is that Professor Gates then shows his ID to show that this is his house and, at that point, he gets arrested for disorderly conduct, charges which are later dropped. . . . I don't know, not having been there and not seeing all the facts, what role race played in that. But I think it's fair to say, number one, any of us would be pretty angry; number two, that the Cambridge police acted stupidly in arresting somebody when there was already proof that they were in their own home; and, number three, what I think we know separate and apart from this incident is that there's a long history in this country of African-Americans and Latinos being stopped by law enforcement disproportionately. That's just a fact. . . . That doesn't lessen the incredible progress we've made. I'm standing here as testimony to that. And yet the fact of the matter is it still haunts us. [2]

This presidential synopsis rallies Obama's followers to meet at the intersection of White Guilt Lane and Black Rage Boulevard. The Black Panther Platform is alive and well in Obama's heart and soul. He poses racism as the primary reason for black males' disproportionate contact with police and their rates of incarceration. No other possibilities enter his social equation. It's "just a fact."

## DEVAL PATRICK

Barack Obama was not alone in postulating racism in the Gates case. Massachusetts Governor Deval Patrick, Massachusetts' first Black governor, exclaimed that Gates' arrest was "every black man's nightmare." Patrick's single mother raised him in the Robert Taylor Homes housing project on the South Side of Chicago. His father, who had a daughter through an affair with another woman, abandoned the family to play jazz in New York City. When he reached high school age, Patrick was given a scholarship to Milton Academy, a prestigious boarding school in Massachusetts.[3] *The Wall Street Journal* (2007) identified Milton as one of the world's top twenty-five schools for preparing students to enter elite American universities. Milton's alumni include TS Eliot, Buckminster Fuller, Robert F. Kennedy, and Ted Kennedy.

After Milton, Patrick advanced to Harvard College and Harvard Law School. He won two Massachusetts gubernatorial contests, serving from 2007–2015. *USA Today* (February 29, 2016) listed Patrick as a possible Obama nominee to fill Antonin Scalia's vacated seat on the US Supreme Court. Name another country where Patrick's story could be replicated. He was the beneficiary of American principles of generosity, benevolence, and unwavering belief in the right to rise. Yet, at the drop of a hat, he impugns the integrity of a Massachusetts police officer and throws down the race card.

## CHARLES JAMES OGLETREE, JR.

Also weighing in for Henry Gates was his lawyer, Charles Ogletree. He earned BA and MA degrees from Stanford, and his JD from Harvard Law School, where he became a professor in 1985. He has moderated television programs including *State of the Black Union* and *Where Do We Go from Here: Chaos or Community.* He taught both Barack and Michelle Obama when they were students at Harvard.[4] Ogletree exploited the Gates-Crowley episode by publishing a book, *The Presumption of Guilt: The Arrest of Henry Louis Gates, Jr., and Race, Class and Crime in America*. The subtitle provides an inkling of the point he wants to make—America is racist and oppresses blacks. In a June 22, 2010, interview on NPR's *Talk of the Nation*, Ogletree declared that race and class were the reasons for this incident getting out of hand. He opined this was "a traditional town/gown problem" where the white working-class police officer clashed with the well-known black Harvard professor. Does that statement make any sense? This seems to be anything but "traditional." It's closer to unheard of.

In prince and pauper fashion, Ogletree described Gates as "one of the nation's leading intellectuals" who is an "esteemed figure on the subjects of race and equality." Crowley was presented as a decent peasant, the product of public schools where he "was successful but not a star student and was well liked by his teachers, coaches, and classmates. He is well respected by his African American former coach at CRLS, George Greenidge . . . (who) states that, to this day, he would swear by Crowley at a moment's notice."[5]

Some Ogletree history is worthy of review. He was caught plagiarizing in *All Deliberate Speed,* a book dealing with the legacy of the Brown v. Board of Education Supreme Court decision ordering school desegregation. Among entries in the *Harvard Plagiarism Archive*, one by Joseph Bottum provides an especially good overview:

> *"Ogletree didn't plan to write All Deliberate Speed in the first place. His graduate assistants cobbled it together for him from other sources—and, as Ogletree puts it, "I was negligent in not overseeing more carefully the final product that carries my name." That's a curious construction, but it seems correct, in the end. Surely we reserve the term 'authors' for people who write books—not people who create 'final products that carry their name.'. . . When did this become the way that a Harvard faculty member produces a book? . . . I find the pseudo-production of All Deliberate Speed [most] disturbing. Ogletree's assistants pasted together material from other books, then swept through the assembled text rewriting, editing, paraphrasing, and summarizing as they went. They got caught because they missed a passage, but what's wrong isn't the part they missed. It's the whole procedure. . . . [B]y every explanation, Ogletree conceived much of the book as a kind of double plagiarism: He set out to put his name on work done by his assistants, who, he knew, were merely rephrasing work written by other people. That is not a book. It is, at the least, tenure-revoking ghostwriting. Why hasn't Harvard, which has known about this for months, done something about Charles Ogletree?"*[6]

This situation with Barack and Michelle Obama's mentor is reviewed because it begs answers to several relevant questions. First, if this Harvard professor lost tenure or was dismissed for plagiarism, what are the chances he would play the race card? Second, did Harvard fear inflammatory racist accusations if they imposed disciplinary sanctions? Third, if confronted, would Harvard have the institutional integrity and fortitude to look into media cameras and say, "Race is irrelevant in this case; we sanctioned Charles Ogletree because he violated fundamental rules of scholarship. We make our judgments based on behavior, not race?"

*The Harvard Crimson*, the school's daily newspaper, formerly edited by Franklin D. Roosevelt, John F. Kennedy, and Michael Crichton, questioned Harvard University's moral character in their September 13, 2004, edition. One of the headlines read, "What academia is hiding: Ogletree's admission of plagiarism speaks to a widespread morally questionable practice." The article discusses "a ludicrous double standard" where there is "glaring disparity in Harvard's plagiarism policies—and the different scholarly standards it holds for its students and faculty." Ogletree admitted that six paragraphs of his book were taken from the work of Yale Law School professor Jack M. Balkin. Ogletree rationalized this plagiarism as an "oversight" due to "strict deadlines" and "reliance on research assistants." The *Crimson* article concludes with this comment:

> *"The bottom line remains that had a Harvard student committed such a grievous error, intentionally or not, the College would likely turn a deaf ear to any excuses—particularly any that involve an over-reliance on paid assistants to do their research and writing for them. If Harvard is not willing to hold its faculty to the same high scholarly standards as it does its students, then perhaps it should rethink its undergraduate plagiarism policy and do away with the charade of irreproachable academic integrity."* [7]

## SERGEANT JAMES CROWLEY'S REPORT

Sgt. James Crowley responded to a reported break-in at Henry Louis Gates' house in a neighborhood that already had twenty-three break-ins, many occurring during the daytime. Crowley's description of events is documented in Cambridge Police Department Incident Report #900127. The bulk of the report is presented verbatim, because it is important to hear his voice and the sequence of events from his perspective:

> *On Thursday June 16, 2009, Henry Gates, Jr. was placed under arrest at -- Ware Street, after being observed exhibiting loud and tumultuous behavior, in a public place, directed at a uniformed police officer who was present investigating a report of a crime in progress. These actions on the behalf of Gates served no legitimate purpose and caused citizens passing this location to stop and take notice while appearing surprised and alarmed. . . .*

> *At approximately 12:44 p.m, I was operating my cruiser on Harvard Street near Ware Street. At that time, I overheard an ECC broadcast for a possible break in progress at — Ware Street. Due to my proximity, I responded. . . .*

> *As I reached the door, a female voice called out to me. I turned and looked in the direction of the voice and observed a white female, later identified as -- -- who was standing on the sidewalk in front of the residence, held a wireless telephone in her hand and told me that it was she who called. She went on to tell me that she observed what appeared to be two black males with backpacks on the porch of — Ware Street. She told me that her suspicions were aroused when she observed one of the men wedging his shoulder into the door as if he was trying to force entry. . . .*

*As I turned and faced the door, I could see an older black male standing in the foyer of — Ware Street. I made this observation through the glass paned front door. As I stood in plain view of this man, later identified as Gates, I asked if he would step out onto the porch and speak with me. He replied no I will not. He then demanded to know who I was. I told him that I was Sgt. Crowley from the Cambridge Police and that I was investigating a report of a break in progress at the residence. While I was making this statement, Gates opened the front door and exclaimed, Why, because I'm a black man in America? I then asked Gates if there was anyone else in the residence. While yelling, he told me that it was none of my business and accused me of being a racist police officer. I assured Gates that I was responding to a citizen's call to the Cambridge Police and that the caller was outside as we spoke. Gates seemed to ignore me and picked up a cordless phone and dialed an unknown telephone number. As he did so, I radioed on channel 1 that I was in the residence with someone who appeared to be a resident but very uncooperative. I then overheard Gates asking the person on the other end of his telephone call to get the chief and what's the chief's name? Gates was telling the person on the other end of the call that he was dealing with a racist police officer in his home. Gates then turned to me and told me that I had no idea who I was messing with and that I had not heard the last of it. While I was led to believe that Gates was lawfully in the residence, I was quite surprised and confused with the behavior he exhibited toward me. I asked Gates to provide me with photo identification so that I could verify that he resided at — Ware Street and so that I could radio my findings to ECC. Gates initially refused, demanding that I show him identification but then did supply me with a Harvard University identification card. . . .*

*With the Harvard University identification in hand, I radioed my finding to ECC on channel two and prepared to leave. Gates again asked for my name which I began to provide. Gates began to yell over my spoken words by accusing me of being a racist police officer and leveling threats that he wasn't someone to mess with. At some point during this exchange, I became aware of Carlos Figueroa standing behind me. When Gates asked a third time for my name, I explained to him that I had provided it at his request two separate times. Gates continued to yell at me. I told Gates that I was leaving his residence and that if he had any other questions regarding the matter, I would speak with him outside of the residence.*

*As I began walking through the foyer toward the front door, I could hear Gates again demanding my name. I again told Gates that I would speak with him outside. My reason for wanting to leave the residence was that Gates was yelling very loud and the acoustics of the kitchen and foyer were making it difficult for me to transmit pertinent information to ECC or other responding units. His reply was ya, I'll speak with your mama outside.'. . .*

*As I descended the stairs to the sidewalk, Gates continued to yell at me, accusing me of racial bias and continued to tell me that I had not heard the last of him. Due to the tumultuous manner Gates had exhibited in his residence as well as his continued tumultuous behavior outside the residence, in view of the public, I warned Gates that he was becoming disorderly. Gates ignored my warning and continued to yell, which drew the attention of both the police officers and citizens, who appeared surprised and alarmed by Gates's outburst. For a second time I warned Gates to calm down while I withdrew my department issued handcuffs from their carrying case. Gates again ignored my warning and continued to yell at me. It was at this time that I informed Gates that he was under arrest. I then stepped up the stairs, onto the porch and attempted to place handcuffs on Gates. Gates initially resisted my attempt to handcuff him, yelling that he was disabled and would fall without his cane. After the handcuffs were properly applied, Gates complained that they were too tight. I ordered Off. Ivey, who was among the responding officers, to handcuff Gates with his arms in front of him for his comfort while I secured a cane for Gates from within the residence. I then asked Gates if he would like an officer to take possession of his house key and secure his front door, which he left wide open. Gates told me that the door was unsecurable due to a previous break attempt at the residence. . . .*

*After a brief consultation with Sgt. Lashley and upon Gates's request, he was transported to 125 6th Street in a police cruiser where he was booked and processed by Officer Crowley.*[8]

Carlos Figueroa, the second officer arriving on the scene, offered this supplement to the report:

*On July 16, 2009 at approximately 12:44 p.m., I Officer Figueroa #509 responded to an ECC broadcast for a possible break at — Ware St. When I arrived, I stepped into the residence and Sgt. Crowley had already entered and was speaking to a black male.*

*As I stepped in, I heard Sgt. Crowley ask for the gentleman's information which he stated NO I WILL NOT! The gentleman was shouting out to the Sgt. that the Sgt. was a racist and yelled that THIS IS WHAT HAPPENS TO BLACK MEN IN AMERICA! As the Sgt. was trying to calm the gentleman, the gentleman shouted You don't know who you're messing with!*

*I stepped out to gather the information from the reporting person. -- -- stated to me that she saw a man wedging his shoulder into the front door as to pry the door open. As I returned to the residence, a group of onlookers were now on the scene. The Sgt., along with the gentleman, were now on the porch of — Ware St., and again he was shouting, now to the onlookers (about seven), THIS IS WHAT HAPPENS TO BLACK MEN IN AMERICA! The gentleman refused to listen to as to why the Cambridge Police were there. While on the porch, the gentleman refused to be cooperative and continued shouting that the Sgt. is a racist police officer.*

## FACTS OF THE MATTER

Among the articles providing meaningful details of this incident were an ABC News report by Michele McPhee and Sara Just (July 22, 2009), and *New York Times* articles by Abby Goodnough (July, 7, 2009, July 23, 2009) and Don VanNatta and Abby Goodnough (July 27, 2009). Information provided by these reporters is used in an effort to understand this event and to evaluate Barack Obama's comments.

Goodnough wrote that Obama seemed to "polarize the national debate." On one side was Cambridge Police Chief Robert Haas who said his officers were "deeply pained" by Obama's comments and added, "We take deep personal pride in this agency." On the other side was the Congressional Black Caucus, demanding that Congress address the issue of racial profiling.[9] This sort of polarization proved to be a defining feature of Barack Obama's two terms in office.

The involved officer, Sgt. James Crowley, was born and raised in the Cambridge area. He wrestled and played football in high school. He was well regarded in his community and had four brothers serving in law enforcement. Crowley joined the Cambridge Police Department in 1998 and was an eleven-year veteran at the time of this incident. Within the department, he was a trusted advisor to the police commissioner. Known for his even temperament, he served as a role model for younger officers. Former Police Commissioner Ronny Watson, who is black, handpicked Crowley to be an instructor at the Lowell Police Academy, teaching fellow officers how to avoid racial profiling. A black lieutenant on the force described Crowley as "stellar."

Obama's explicit indictment of Crowley and implicit indictment of America's police drew strong reaction from law enforcement. Jim Carnell, union representative for the Boston Police Patrolmen's Association, stated that police were "furious at the way Crowley is being vilified." He explained his sentiments:

> *"The officer's mindset when going in there is, "Why was he breaking down the door?" Maybe there is a restraining order in place. Maybe Harvard University, who owns the house, changed the locks for some reason. The officer's job is to make sure everything is on the up-and-up."*

> *Mr. Gates should be grateful that the police responded and explained himself with some civil discourse. . . . It would have ended there. Instead, his arrogant, combative behavior gave the cops cause to wonder that something else was going on."[10]*

Hugh Cameron, president of the Massachusetts Coalition of Police, offered the following summary:

> *"The actions of the Cambridge Police Department, and in particular, Sgt. Crowley, were 100 percent correct. He was responding to a report of two men breaking into a home. The police cannot just drive by the house and say, Looks like everything is OK. Sgt. Crowley was carrying out his duty as a law enforcement officer protecting the property of Professor Gates, and he was accused of being a racist. The situation would have been over in five minutes if Professor Gates cooperated with the officer. Unfortunately, the situation we are in now is the environment police work in now."[11]* (Author's note: this is an environment made more dangerous and less gratifying by Barack Obama.)

During interviews, Crowley stated that he remained calm and never raised his voice while interacting with Gates. He was surprised when the professor refused to step outside and described Gates as oddly belligerent from the start: "From the time he opened the door it seemed that he was very upset, very put off that I was there in the first place. Not just what he said, but the tone in which he said it, just seemed very peculiar—even more so now that I know how educated he is." He explained that Gates "was arrested after following me outside the house and continuing the tirade even after being warned multiple times—probably a few more times than the average person would have gotten. He was cautioned in the house, 'Calm down, lower your voice'." Crowley added, "The professor at any point in time could have resolved the issue by quieting down and/or by going back in the house." [12] With regard to the issue of racism, he said, "No one that knows me thought that the arrest was based on race in any way. Arrests are based strictly on behavior."[13]

Crowley explained his thought process by stating, "I didn't know who he was. I was by myself. I was the only police officer standing there, and I got a report that there were people breaking into a house." Asking Gates to step outside "was for my safety first and foremost. I have to go home at night to three beautiful children and a wife who depend on me."[14]

Henry Louis Gates' side of the story indicates that he arrived home after a fourteen-hour flight from China, sick with bronchitis, on Thursday June 16, 2009. He was "bewildered" because his front door was jammed from a break-in attempt. Gates asked the cab driver who brought him from the airport, a burly, dark-skinned Moroccan, to help him with the door. The cabbie shouldered the door open.

Gates' lawyer, Charles Ogletree, said that after getting into the house, Gates called Harvard's maintenance department to come fix the door. He then saw Sgt. Crowley on his porch. According to Ogletree, Crowley was disrespectful from the beginning, asking the professor to step outside without explanation and demanding identification. When Crowley did not seem to believe Gates lived "a few blocks from Harvard Square," Gates became frustrated and asked for the officer's name and badge number, which Crowley repeatedly refused to provide. During an interview on the *Today* show, Gates said:

> *"I demanded to know his name and his badge number. He wouldn't say anything. He was just very upsetting, and I said, "Why are you not responding to me? Are you not responding to me because you're a white police officer and I'm a black man?" He turned his back on me, walked out, I followed him onto my porch. It looked like a police convention, there were so many policeman outside. I stepped out on my porch and said, "I want to know your colleague's name and his badge number," and this officer said "Thank you for accommodating my earlier request, you are under arrest." Look how tumultuous I am. I'm five foot seven. I weigh 150 pounds and my tumultuous, outrageous action was to demand that he give me his name and his badge number (The person seated next to Gates burst into laughter, tacitly*

*supporting the notion of his victimhood.).* "[15]

This Gates commentary is telling. It verifies Crowley's description of events. Crowley claimed that after making his initial call to alert ECC that he had contact with an individual whom he thought was the resident, Gates went on such a loud and sustained verbal tirade that Crowley could not hear input on his police radio. When the dispatcher heard the commotion and received no responses from Crowley over the radio, more police were sent to the scene. The fact that six additional cars had enough time to arrive before Gates and Crowley stepped onto the porch indicates the ruckus inside was not brief. It also was reported that Crowley had his mike open during this time. If the police radio recording supported Gates' story, it would have been a national headline. Ogletree's comments showed that he was yearning for a lawsuit. Instead, political pressure was brought to bear, and that tape was never made public.

During email correspondence with the media, Gates said that he used no racial slurs, profanity, or threats. He added, "But I do not believe that standing up for my rights as a citizen should be against the law." He concluded, "I think that Sergeant Crowley has backed himself in a very tight corner, and I think that is most unfortunate. My offer to listen to a heartfelt and credible apology is a sincere one, and continues to stand."[17]

Gates' *Today* interview convinced me that he was lying. I believe he painted himself into a very tight corner. He spun a tale that was rationalized as truth because it was the sequence of events from his perspective. This mimics Ogletree's rationalizations regarding his plagiarism. It is reminiscent of Viron's sworn testimony in the Darren Wilson case. Facts be damned. No need for the Harvard professor to worry about impugning the integrity of Officer Crowley or the law enforcement community.

## ANALYZING OBAMA'S COMMENTS

*Obama Comment One:* "I think it is fair to say, number one, any of us would be pretty angry" (if a police officer arrived at our house and asked for identification).

This statement reflects the magnitude of Obama's shallow racist thinking. There are many who believe his messages, accepting the rhetorical use of words like "fair," "fact," and "truth" as gospel. Let's take a critical look. What would "any of us" do under the circumstances? Common sense says that we would be on alert if (a) there were twenty-three break-ins in our neighborhood, (b) someone jimmied our door while attempting to break it, and (c) we arrived home after a long trip to a jimmied door. Under such circumstances, most of us would be happy to see police patrolling our street and even standing on our porch. Furthermore, we might suspect that a concerned neighbor would alert police if our front door was just shouldered open by a "burly Moroccan" who was a stranger in the neighborhood. Providing identification would be totally understandable and even appreciated. Our first question to the officer might be "What's up?" or "How can I help?" We wouldn't jump to inferences about racism if the officer didn't match our demographic. Obama propagating the belief that "any of us would be pretty angry" is based on something other than circumstances.

Gates' friends told the *New York Times* "that perhaps his fatigue, his illness, and his bewilderment at having an officer question his presence in his own home combined to make him lose his characteristic cool."[18] What other possibilities come to mind? Was he taking medication that made him edgy? Did he drink too much alcohol on the flight home? Was he just tired, irritable, and grumpy? Who knows? Something was off, and I don't believe it was Sergeant Crowley's attitude.

*Obama Comment Two*: "My understanding is that Professor Gates then shows his ID to show that this is his house and, at that point, he gets arrested for disorderly conduct, charges which are later dropped."

First, Gates was not arrested in his house. He was cuffed outside after following Crowley onto the porch and verbally abusing him in front of multiple witnesses. The issue of when and how Gates presented ID is debatable. The crucial element is Obama's phrase, "charges which were later dropped." This insinuates the charges were bogus, lends support to Gates' version of events, and reinforces the impression that Crowley acted stupidly. There is a more detailed and factual explanation of how and why the charges were dropped.

A high-ranking official in the Cambridge Police Department told ABC News, "Let's face it, this case has nothing to do with race. This is a man who has made some phone calls and the case went away. They treated him with kid gloves. Harvard University executives rushed to the police station to monitor the entire situation. They let him off the hook. The mayor threw the department under the bus. She might as well open the city's checkbook. . . . If Professor Gates was poor, he'd be in a jail cell."[19]

Former prosecutor David Frank said it was unusual for a case to be "nul-processed" (charges dropped) without a court appearance. Frank explained, "Legally, the prosecution made the right call. The issue, though, is that if Gates were an electrician from Everett and not a well-known professor from Harvard, the reality is that in all likelihood he would have to defend himself against the charges in a courtroom. He never stepped into a courtroom and the charges were dropped."[20]

Gerry Leone of the Middlesex County District Attorney's Office claimed political influence played no role in this case. He said a complaint "can be dropped at any time." It was Leone who brokered the meeting between Ogletree and the police department to see "if the case could be resolved." Obama never hinted that phone calls were made, that Harvard rushed in, that Gates was treated with kid gloves, or that the case "went away" in a highly politicized manner.

The mayor accused of throwing the police department under the bus was E. Denise Simmons. She was elected to office in the Harvard-dominated city of Cambridge, Massachusetts, which is 66.6 percent White, 15.1 percent Asian or Pacific Islander, 11.7 percent Black, and 6.6 percent Hispanic, according to the 2010 U.S. census. Simmons is an openly homosexual black female. Her resume indicates that she came into power through being a community organizer. She spent twelve years with the Civic Unity Committee, a city-funded "citizen rights" organization. A major project for Simmons was increasing faculty diversity in the Cambridge school system. She won election to city council in 2001 and dedicated herself to assuring that black, GLBT, and female constituencies were "given a voice" in city hall. Other projects included helping local minority business owners establish themselves in Cambridge and initiating conversations about the role of race and class in the community. She returned to City Council following her 2008–2009 term as mayor, but reassumed the office of mayor on January 4, 2016. [21]

*Obama Comment Three*: "What I think we know separate and apart from this incident is that there's a long history in this country of African Americans and Latinos being stopped by law enforcement disproportionately. That's just a fact. . . . That doesn't lessen the incredible progress we've made. I'm standing here as testimony to that. And yet the fact of the matter is it still haunts us."

Obama ignores crime and homicide statistics such those in St. Louis during 2015 (173 black murder victims, 112 back suspects; 15 white murder victims, 3 white suspects). If we apply common sense realism, this level of devastation in the black community should be primary in Obama's social equation. Add the number of wounded and injured to this death toll, and the level of required police involvement required in the black community is tremendous. Read the comments of people in the cities of St. Louis or Chicago who lament what is happening around them. Take the police out of the equation and Charles Barkley's prediction that black neighborhoods would turn into the Wild West seems plausible. For Obama, Niggas wit Attitude's mantra of "*f*ck tha police*" is never posed as a factor inspiring black males' oppositional and defiant behavior that escalates into violence. According to him, police act stupidly. They don't know how to relate to "communities of color." "That's just a fact" in his perception. Echoes of Bernie Sanders ring in my ears.

Many of us are saddened rather than haunted by the level of violence in too many black communities where good people are fearful on their streets and in their homes. We grieve when thinking of eleven-year-old Antonio Johnson getting shot in the head while learning how to spell the word "unsafe." We cringe at the thought of someone shooting Deandre Joshua in the head, dousing him with gasoline, and setting him on fire while he sat in his car near the intersection where Michael Brown died. We are frustrated by "crabs in a barrel" negating the American principle of the right to rise.

## REACTIONS TO THE INCIDENT

The July 20, 2009, issue of *Yale Daily News* announced that Al Sharpton planned to attend Gates' arraignment. He exclaimed, "This arrest is indicative of at best police abuse of power or at worst the highest example of racial profiling I have seen. I have heard of driving while black and even shopping while black but now even going to your own home while black is a new low in police-community affairs."[22] Because someone made a call and the case went away, there was no arraignment. There was no basis to sue Crowley or his police department. Sharpton missed a terrific opportunity.

Kelly King, a black female officer on the Cambridge Police Department, spoke about the case during a CNN interview. She indicated, "There has been a rush to judgment." She reported, "I think professor Gates has done a very good job of throwing up a very effective smoke screen called 'racist' that had nothing to do with it." The interviewer then asked what she thought of President Obama. Her reply was, "It's unfortunate. I supported him. I voted for him. I will not again." She concluded by saying that people around the country should, "Keep their minds open and realize that we would not support someone that we felt wronged someone else. We took this job to do the right thing. We all took this job to do the right thing. We would not support anyone in blue doing the wrong thing."[23] Although he was present, James Crowley was not allowed to speak. The interview ended with an embrace between him and Kelly King.

No case could do a better job of refuting the claim that America operates on racist principles than the Gates-Crowley confrontation. If anything, it resoundingly proves the opposite. President Obama wants us to be "haunted." If we aren't, we are racists. In reality, James Crowley is a middle class white police officer who had to withstand vilification from his black mayor who was elected in a town where 11.7 percent of the population was black, his black governor who was elected by a state where 6.6 percent of the population was black, and his black president who was elected by a country where 12.6 percent of the population was black (2010 statistics). How would this be possible if America was the land of racial animus and oppression portrayed by President Obama, his mentor Charles Ogletree, and his advisor Al Sharpton?

In the face of these overwhelming odds, James Crowley would not shrink and did not blink. He calmly stated he is not a racist, he did nothing wrong, he enforced the law fairly, and he will *never* apologize for making an arrest that was justified. He said the arrest was exclusively the product of the professor's behavior. When asked about Obama's comments, he said, "I think he was way off base wading into a local issue without knowing all the facts."[24] Those who know Crowley best verify that he is a good cop and no racist; both blacks and whites in his community swear to it. With regard to his unwavering stance, one of his friends explained, "The professor didn't know who *he* was messing with."[25] I want Jimmy Crowley in my foxhole if I go into battle.

Obama's comments generated tremendous public backlash. When asked about this, he replied, "You know, I have to say that I'm surprised by the controversy surrounding my statements because I think it was a pretty straightforward commentary that you probably don't have to handcuff a guy, a middle-aged man, who uses a cane, who is in his own home. I think it doesn't make sense, with all the problems we have out there, to arrest a guy in his own home if he is not causing a serious disturbance."[26] Gates continues to be held harmless and Crowley still has no credibility in Obama's narrative. We should believe him because he wants us to believe that what he says is "straightforward."

By July 25, 2009, the *New York Times* indicated that Obama was forced to backpedal in an effort to defuse the volatile national debate. He said, "I obviously helped to contribute ratcheting it up. I want to make clear that in my choice of words, I think I unfortunately gave an impression that I was maligning the Cambridge Police Department or Sergeant Crowley specifically, and I could have calibrated those words differently."[27] Thank you, Barack Obama. Now we know that he wasn't wrong, it was just that his language needed a little recalibration. The *New York Times* explained the matter further:

> *"Mr. Obama's unusual personal intervention and public statement came just four hours after the White House said he had no more to say on the matter. But after talking with Michelle Obama and some of his closest friends amid unrelenting publicity, his advisers said, the president reversed course in hopes of quashing a dispute that had set off strong reactions and made it*

*harder for the White House to focus attention on his efforts to pass health care legislation."* [28]

## THE TEACHABLE MOMENT/BEER SUMMIT

Following a nine-month investigation of the case, which the June 30, 2010, *Washington Post* claimed was "fed by a combustible mix of race, class, respect and police authority,"[29] the committee released its findings in a report titled, "Missed Opportunities, Shared Responsibilities." The document said both individuals contributed to the outcome unintentionally. Both had opportunities to ratchet down the encounter. Both looked at the same set of circumstances from different perspectives. Both had a certain degree of fear of each other. These, most certainly, are conclusions drafted by political committee.

President Obama invited Gates and Crowley to the White House for an informal meeting over beers intended to be a "teachable moment" on race that would provide "an opportunity to listen to each other." Obama, Gates, Crowley, and Vice President Joe Biden gathered in the Rose Garden outside the White House. The *New York Times* explained, "The addition of Mr. Biden was interesting, for a number of reasons. Mr. Biden was able to draw on his credibility with blue-collar, labor union America and his roots in Scranton, PA, to add balance to the photo op that the White House presented: two black guys, two white guys, sitting around a table." [30] Gates and Crowley both wore suits and ties, while Obama and Biden were look-alikes with dark slacks and white starched shirts with the sleeves rolled up. Obama was the only one slouched in his chair, projecting a casual air. After the meeting, Gates said, "I don't think anybody but Barack Obama would have thought about bringing us together." Crowley summarized, "What you had today was two gentlemen who agreed to disagree on a particular issue."[31]

## RESPONSE OF ELIZABETH GATES

As with everything else in this case, the teachable moment/beer summit drew reactions. Gates' daughter, Elizabeth Gates, wrote her view in an article for the *Daily Beast.* She called the meeting "a circus-like ending of a misunderstanding between a couple of very decent men." With regard to the host, she stated, "I saw Mr. Obama's lean body cooly draped over a lawn chair." She rendered the judgment that "Crowley's not a bad guy."[32]

However, her article had the same prince and pauper condescending air as Charles Ogletree's book. She described the Crowley's as "a pleasant family of five," then turned a critical eye on family members. She said, "I first caught sight of Crowley's lovely daughter; she was wearing an appropriately heavy and charmingly untrained amount of green eyeliner on her lower lashes, and I saw my former self in her." She emphasized her father's social savvy and superiority by describing the initial encounter with the Crowleys in the White House She said, "True to form, my father cut right through the thick tension of hurried salutations and offered the Sergeant his hand and joked, 'You looked bigger the last time I saw you.' Crowley's cheeks flushed red as a smile dashed across his lips, and his young son, whose cheeks had long since flushed the same muted crimson, looked up at his father and smiled." She determined, "This wasn't a family raised on hate."

Through all of this, there was a socio-political point to be made. She concluded with the following statement:

> "Discrimination is the single greatest wound in American history and could never be solved over a beer. Not today, not tomorrow, not ever. There are more black men in prison than in college and literally thousands of black men are arrested across this country each day. And while I might agree with the president's initial statement that the Cambridge Police Department acted stupidly, my father is not the first nor will he be the last black man to be arrested for no reason—in his own home or elsewhere—and Sergeant Crowley isn't the first officer to fudge a police report. They are simply pawns in the rebirth of unfashionable intolerance in a world that likes to think our dashing brown-skinned forty-fourth president has emerged to make nice with the past, present, and future.... As my father said on the plane yesterday morning on our way to the White House, there are approximately 800,000 black men in prison and on July 16, 2009, I simply became one of them."

Oh, I get it. The bottom line is that her father is an innocent victim, one of 800,000 innocent black victims. Black men are jailed as the direct result of our nation's vulnerable value system. Her father had the misfortune of living in a country that discriminates. It is unfeasible that the most meaningful discrimination in his life (or hers for that matter) worked in his favor as he ascended the elite educational ladder to fulfill the American dream cherished by so many during an era of affirmative action. That decent man with muted crimson cheeks from the pleasant family of five is a liar, serving as a pawn within a law enforcement community of liars. Now, and in the future, we must hang the audacity of our hopes on the dashing, brown-skinned president. I classify Elizabeth Gates' commentary as condescending and distorted.

## RESPONSE OF VAN JONES

Van Jones was a powerful advisor to Barack Obama at the time of this meeting. *Breitbart News* reported comments he made on the *Democracy Now* TV show. Jones declared the meeting was a "terrifying, shocking" revelation about the state of race relations in America that forced the President to "sit humbly" across from a "racist" police officer. He elaborated:

> *"The right wing and the law enforcement establishment brought the wrath of God down on the White House, I was there, and suddenly he's forced to do a beer summit to sit eye to eye with a racist police officer . . . as a black man, even the most powerful man in the world, he cannot speak about race and if he does he's then forced to sit humbly across the table from a racist police officer."* [33]

When looking at vitriolic statements, it is always worth considering the source. Van Jones was born in Jackson, Tennessee, received a BS. from the University of Tennessee at Martin, and then a law degree from Yale in 1993. During 1992, he was arrested while demonstrating as a volunteer legal monitor for a San Francisco protest of the Rodney King verdict. He claimed "the incident deepened my disaffection with the system and accelerated my political radicalization." By August 1992, he declared himself a communist. Over the ensuing years he participated in a number of groups including: Standing Together to Organize a Revolutionary Movement (STORM), a "socialist collective" protesting police brutality; Color of Change, an organization for strengthening black America's political voice; and, the Green-Collar Jobs Campaign, intended to improve racial and economic equality while addressing environmental concerns—creating "green pathways out of poverty." In a curious hodgepodge of socio-political verbiage, Jones posed that environmental justice and environmental racism could be addressed through conservation, regulation and investment.

On October 7, 2008, Jones published a book, *The Green Dollar Economy*, which received positive reviews from Al Gore and Nancy Pelosi. Jones became the first black author to make the *New York Times* bestseller list with an environmental book. On March 10, 2009, Barack Obama appointed Jones to serve as Special Advisor for Green Jobs, Enterprise and Innovation at the White House Council on Environmental Quality. He was dubbed Obama's *Green Jobs Czar*. Jones resigned on September 5, 2009 when his past was illuminated and criticized in the media, particularly by Glenn Beck who listed the following concerns about Jones:

- He's a communist revolutionary

- He defended and helped coordinate the 1999 protest march on behalf of Mumia Abu-Jamal (the convicted killer of Philadelphia police officer Daniel Faulkner) .

- He believes the free market is dead.

- He signed the 9/11 Truth Commission petition that called for an inquiry into government officials' involvement in the September 11 terrorist attacks.

- In January, 2008, he claimed white polluters were steering poison into the communities of people of color,

- He wants a green economy to replace a system of oppression and exploitation [34]

WorldNetDaily (WND) offered the following revelations:

- Jones said he first became radicalized in the wake of the 1992 Rodney King riots, during which time he was arrested. "I was a rowdy nationalist on April 28th, and then the verdicts came down on April 29th," he said. "By August, I was a communist." "I met all these young radical people of color—I mean really radical: communists and anarchists. And it was, like, 'This is what I need to be a part of.' I spent the next ten years of my life working with a lot of those people I met in jail, trying to be a revolutionary."

- One day after the 9/11 attacks, Jones led a vigil that expressed solidarity with Arab and Muslim Americans as well as what he called the victims of 'US. imperialism' around the world.

- Days before his White House appointment, Jones used a forum at a major youth convention to push for a radical agenda that included spreading the wealth and "changing the whole system."

- Jones' Maoist manifesto while leading the group Standing Together to Organize a Revolutionary Movement was scrubbed from the Internet after being revealed by WND.

- Jones was the main speaker at an anti-war rally that urged "resistance" against the US government—a demonstration sponsored by an organization associated with the Revolutionary Communist Party.

- In a 2005 conference, Jones characterized the US. as an "apartheid regime" that civil rights workers helped turn into a "struggling, fledgling democracy."[35]

This is the man Obama selected for a position of leadership in his administration. What happened to this communist/anarchist, anti-US government, anti-police, promoter of white conspiracy theories who beats the drum of oppression and exploitation and blames his ouster from the White House on a "vicious smear campaign?" In 2010, Princeton University, the school built on the principles of Scotch-Irish Common Sense Realism, gave him the position of distinguished visiting fellow in both the Center for African American Studies and the program in Science, Technology and Environmental Policy at the Woodrow Wilson School of Public and International Affairs. In 2011, Jones launched "Rebuild the Dream," an advocacy project intended "to give the progressive mass movement that rose up to elect Barack Obama a new banner to march under." In June 2013, CNN hired him to co-host their political debate show, *Crossfire*, along with Newt Gingrich, Stephanie Cutter, and S. E. Cupp. The show was canceled in October 2014.[36]

In 2014, Jones founded Dream Corps and provided the slogan, "Twenty-first century jobs, not jails." Their website reads like a treatise in megalomania. They claim to help "cutting-edge initiatives grow big enough to impact millions of lives." Their "shared platform helps leaders create synergies, leapfrog obstacles and maximize impact." Dream Corps has three major components:

1. #YesWeCode aims to "increase opportunity in the tech sector." Their major goal is to help 100,000 young women and men from low-opportunity backgrounds find success in the tech sector.
2. #Cut50 aims to "transform the criminal justice system." Their major goal is to reduce our incarcerated population by 50 percent over the next ten years.
3. #GreenforAll aims to "build an inclusive green economy." Their major goal is to move $1 trillion from polluters pockets into low-income communities.

The Dream Corps website presents the following "highlights" in their *2015 End of Year Report*:

- Prince concert launches # YesWeCode.
- Bipartisan summit generates three criminal justice bills.
- #GreenForAll works with White House to deliver solar benefits to low-income Americans.

- #YesWeCode partners with the White House, Essence Magazine, and MSNBC to connect youth to computer training.

- #JusticeReformNOW campaign collects nearly 250,000 signatures, including 100+ celebrities like Stephen Curry and Amy Schumer.

- African American church leaders join forces with the US Green Building Council and Green For All to launch "Green the Church."

- #YesWeCode launches national job training pilot in Oakland, California.

- #cut50 team works closely with the White House, Congress and Newt Gingrich to advance legislation.

- Green For All defends Obama's "Clear Power Plan" for polluter attacks.

- Vien Truong joins Green For All as National Director.

What do we notice about these highlights? (a) They seem to describe the strategies of a lobbying firm intended to milk the system that Jones wants to overthrow. (b) They reference Obama or the White House in four of the ten highlights. (c) They mention the notable alliance with the White House, Essence Magazine, and MSNBC. (d) They demonstrate no hint of objective accountability regarding where this nonprofit's money is spent or the level of program effectiveness. It seems likely that the "criminal justice bills" deal with releasing prisoners rather than eliminating the causes of criminality.

Glenn Beck said his criticism was never about Jones' agenda, it was about the agenda of Barack Obama. Beck commented, "There are those in the highest offices in the land who are trying to fundamentally transform this country." During a July 28, 2009, edition of *Fox & Friends*, he labeled Obama as a "racist" with a "deep-seated hatred for white people." He commented that Obama's hiring of Jones, whom he called a "black nationalist who is also an avowed communist," serves as proof that his accusation is true.

## RESPONSE OF CHRIS MATHEWS

Sergeant James Crowley held a fifteen-minute news conference following the teachable moment/beer summit. He answered every question and managed the media with noteworthy poise. The interview is worth watching on YouTube to get a feel for the man. *Hardball* offered the following post-interview commentary:

Chris Mathews: After that remarkable press conference, I have watched politicians for about forty years now. He's better than most of them."

Roger Simon: Is this guy suave or what, "We had a cordial and productive discussion," he's like a head of state.

Matthews: He answered a lot of questions, no apologies, he said they're going to look forward. They are going to have a meaningful discussion later, not over a beer, but a serious get-together.

Mark Whitaker: I think we've seen that a star is born. I think this guy could have a future in politics and the media, we'll see.

Matthews: Look out Deval Patrick in the next election, the governor up there. I have to tell you, I feel like we're watching *Britain's Got Talent*. . . . We've got our Susan Boyle here.

Watching Officer James Crowley after wading through Van Jones' philosophies and activities was like emerging from a dark, dank, labyrinth into a sunlit meadow. William Holmes McGuffey had the correct formula for shaping values. The best of our humanity emerges from common sense principles of morality. These characteristics are evident in Crowley, a stand-up husband, father, friend, cop, and contributing member of his community. He lives the principles on which our nation was built. Thank you for your service, Sergeant Crowley. Harvard and Princeton seem to have strayed from the moral vision of their founders. They now devote themselves to socio-political constructs and cower at the thought of being politically incorrect

# CHAPTER 7

# WHAT'S BARACK OBAMA ALL ABOUT?
# - COMPARE AND CONTRAST

My intention when writing this book was to restore common sense to the discussion of right, wrong, and race in America. This task begins with understanding the principles necessary to develop productive citizens and effective communities. Principles are essential to hold society together, to reduce human suffering, and to identify and solve problems in ways that are fair and just.

Problems can never be solved if you begin with the wrong principles and generate faulty hypotheses. Politicians, including Barack Obama and Bernie Sanders, make this mistake when they posit that America operates according to racist principles and then distort facts and circumstances to support their point of view. You don't have to look far to see why they are wrong. Refugees would not flock to our borders from every corner of the world if America was the oppressive racist entity they portray. Here are unsolicited testimonials from two individuals who shared their stories with me. These personal anecdotes support the notion that America's primary principle is *the right to rise* – regardless of race

Following my cancer surgery, the evening duty nurse was Vietnamese. She came to America alone, speaking no English, with few contacts. She eventually made her way to the Philadelphia area where she joined the housekeeping staff in a hospital. She improved her English, went to school, and is now a nurse. She married a white man and has three children; two are in college and one is doing well in high school. She expressed gratitude for the efforts of American troops in Vietnam as well as the opportunities afforded in America that would be impossible in her country.

The second story comes from a cab driver in Denver. He immigrated to the United States from the chronically war-torn nation of Eritrea in East Africa. He came to this country with few resources and worked his way up to owning his own cab, a luxurious Chevy Tahoe. He is married, has a lovely home, and speaks proudly of his two daughters who are excellent students. He also shared thanks, volunteering that "anyone who works hard can be successful in America." He did and he is.

The simple truth is that the path to personal and social prosperity is good citizenship. The educator survey in Chapter 2 indicates that good citizenship requires: respect and responsibility; motivation, self-control, and compliance; and, family involvement and supervision. These elements should serve as benchmarks for raising children. they also should be in the forefront when assessing behavior and events. Throughout our history, the principles on which America was founded have afforded more opportunity for good citizens than any other nation in the world. That was true in 1788 and it remains true today.

The concept of "good citizenship" has lost some of its clout and prominence. The 1960s were highlighted earlier in this book because socio-political inclinations spawned by the anti-war, civil rights, and Great Society movements continue to have tremendous impact. Here is their downside to those movements. First, they discourage patriotism and gratitude (qualities that stimulate optimism and a sense of "we"); second, they encourage criticism and protest (qualities that generate pessimism and animosity); and, third, they devalue belief in personal responsibility, shifting responsibility for any personal or social failure onto agencies other than individuals.

To further explore Barack Obama's presidential legacy, I want to take a closer look at his underlying beliefs and how they fit with objective notions of good citizenship. He is clearly an advocate of principles derived from the 60s, which were instilled in him by his mother whom he described as an advocate of "position-paper liberalism." Obama consistently labels America's operational principles as unfair, unjust, and racist. When dealing with dysfunction in "communities of color," he identifies the villain as our "system." Which typically translates to police, the criminal justice establishment, or educators. He consistently demonstrates racist bias when judging individual behavior and social events, while shunning objective, ethical criteria.

To further clarify Obama's beliefs and political stance, I use the content of his May 7, 2016, commencement speech at Howard University.[1] He is an effective public speaker. This address is worth watching because it provides an excellent example of both his style and his mindset. His underlying premise is that all "gaps" between blacks and whites are the product of a system that is unjust and unfair.

To offer a contrast to Obama, I compare his views with those of Jason L. Riley, a journalist who is a senior fellow at the Manhattan Institute. Riley's primary social criticisms relate to specific behaviors, and the social and political forces promoting them. He is a strong advocate of personal responsibility

Riley's opinions come from his 2014 book, *Please Stop Helping Us: How Liberals Make It Harder for Blacks to Succeed.*[2] Riley looks at black culture and posits the harmful effects of liberal policies and programs started during the 1960s. He also shares a personal, street-level view of his experiences as a black man in America.

The contrasting views of these two men are presented in distinct categories. Riley's views are mostly paraphrased, with page number references placed in parentheses to show where the ideas are found in his book. It is interesting to note that Riley's comments (2014) precede Obama's speech (2016) by two years. The continuing relevance of Riley's critique shows the predictability of Obama's message over time.

## BARACK OBAMA AND JASON L. RILEY: COMPARE AND CONTRAST

### Justice and Fairness

Obama:

- Even as we each embrace our own beautiful, unique, and valid versions of our blackness, remember the tie that does bind us as African-Americans - and that is our particular awareness of *injustice, and unfairness, and struggle*.

Riley:

- The black underclass struggles because of *values and habits*, not injustice. The idea that racism hinders blacks is a maneuver to blame whites or society for "self-inflicted wounds." (p. 33) Riley asserts that most civil rights leaders and black politicians encourage blacks to see themselves as victims, blaming white racism for causing black pathology. (p. 46)

### Responsibility for Personal Achievement

Obama:

- Obama stated that his "pet peeve" was that "People who have been successful and don't realize they've been lucky. That God may have blessed them; it wasn't nothin' you did. So don't have an attitude."

Riley:

- Riley pointed out that Obama, in a January 2014 interview with *New Yorker* magazine, disparaged Booker T. Washington's (1856-1915) up-by-the-bootstraps message that, in Obama's words, "let the larger society off the hook." (p. 20) Washington, founder of Alabama's Tuskegee Institute, believed that education and entrepreneurship was the key to black progress. He believed self-determination for blacks could be achieved through industry, skill, economy, intelligence, and character. (p. 18) Washington encouraged blacks to develop an identity for hard-work, intelligence, and patriotism, "not for being aggrieved." (p. 21)

## Economic Opportunity

Obama:

- We still got a big gap with economic opportunity. The overall unemployment rate is 5%, but the black unemployment rate is almost 9 percent.

Riley:

- Black unemployment in 1930, in an era of open racial discrimination, was lower than that of whites. In 1950, the unemployment rate for young black men was similar to that of young white men. (p. 101) Riley attributes the current unemployment situation to social programs, especially Lyndon Johnson's Great Society, that undermine the work ethic and promote fatherless homes. (p. 4) He points out that 70 percent of black children are born to unwed mothers and only 16 percent of black households consist of married couples with children. (p. 37) In his view, one of the most important lessons derived from the Obama presidency is that "having a black man in the Oval Office is less important than having one in the home." (p. 33)

## Achievement

Obama:

- We still got an achievement gap. Black boys and girls graduate from high school and college at lower rates than white boys and white girls.

Riley:

- Riley speaks of the coarsening of black culture, particularly the negative influence of rap with its vulgarity and antisocial messages. As mentioned previously, Chuck D of Public Enemy talked about chaos in classroom once "rappers came in the game." They created a "confusing element" encouraging kids to have a, "Yo, f**k this" attitude. (p. 51) Riley expresses the concern that: "A culture that takes pride in ignorance and mocks learnedness has a dim future." (p. 50) He outlines how black immigrants from countries such as Ethiopia, Eritrea, and Somalia outperform black American students (p. 48). Asians (a racial minority in America never thrown into Obama's discussion of social issues such as family, education, and crime) tend to place a high value on education and encourage one another to do well. Proof of how this plays out in the real world is seen in the eight specialized high schools in New York City. Of the 14,400 students in these schools, half are Asian, even though Asians comprise only 14 percent of the public school enrollment (p. 49). Riley comments, "So while multiculturalists are busy complaining about teaching methods and civil rights leaders are busy complaining about standardized tests, the Asian kids are busy studying" (p. 50).

## Black Kids Who Don't Succeed

Obama:

- We have cousins and uncles and brothers and sisters who we remember were just as smart and just as talented as we were, but somehow got ground down by structures that are unfair and unjust.

Riley:

- Riley observed many of his black peers, even those from good families, who "chose to reject middle-class values" of good citizenship. These individuals were not "ground down by structures that are unfair and unjust." Their choices led them to become victims of "social pathologies" such as addiction, criminality, and teen pregnancy. Riley's family moved from a predominantly black to a predominantly white neighborhood because his father did not like what the "knuckleheads" and "thugs" were doing to their own community. Being a "bookish" kid, he found himself ridiculed by black peers for "acting white." (p. 41)

## Criminal Justice

Obama:

- We've got a justice gap when too many black boys and girls pass through a pipeline from underfunded schools to overcrowded jails. This is one area where things have gotten worse. When I was in college about a half a million people in America were behind bars; today there are about 2.2 million. Black men are about six times likelier to be in prison right now than white men.

Riley:

- Again, in sharp contrast to Obama, Riley comments that more blacks are in prison because they "are responsible for an astoundingly disproportionate number of crimes." Furthermore, most victims of black crime are black. He shares the fact that more than ninety percent of black murder victims in 2007 were killed by another black. (p. 78)

## The "Civil Rights" Movement

Obama:

- He (Dr. King) also sat down with President Johnson in the Oval Office to try to get a Civil Rights Act and a Voting Rights Act passed. And those two seminal bills were not perfect just like the Emancipation Proclamation was a war document as much as it was some clarion call for freedom. Those mileposts of our progress were not perfect. They did not make up for centuries of slavery or Jim Crow or eliminate racism or provide for 40 acres and a mule.

Riley:

- Riley described Obama as perpetuating a tradition that has been prevalent since the 1960s, ignoring antisocial black culture while blaming all ailments in black communities on the legacy of slavery. Riley feels, "The civil rights movement has become an industry that does little more than monetize white guilt." (p. 172)

## CONCLUSION

Comparing and contrasting the beliefs of Barack Obama and Jason L. Riley is important because they differ markedly know how they define social problems; and, they point in dramatically different directions with regard to finding solutions.

Obama wants to change the American system, which he repeatedly describes as unfair, unjust, and racist. For him, responsibility for social ills belongs to the system. Riley, on the other hand, wants to change behavior and a subculture that propagates antisocial behavior and fosters what he sees as a tragic, socially self-defeating cycle. For him, responsibility belongs to the individual and community. In the terms of Thomas Reid's philosophy of Common Sense Realism, Obama promotes the notion of "necessity," suggesting that prejudicial outside forces are responsible for creating "gaps" between whites and blacks. Riley could be described as an advocate of "moral liberty," proposing that all people have to discern right from wrong, merit from demerit, and establish moral first principles. Their choices will define both the direction and the quality of their lives. For him, the challenge for blacks is identifying and overcoming self-imposed barriers.

I believe Barack Obama's approach to our social challenges at the national level has been as ineffective as his approach as a community organizer in Chicago where he focused on minor projects while thousands of blacks were murdered in the streets and good citizens cried out for help. While the Chicago's schools fought an uphill battle to provide quality education, he sent his daughters to private school where they were segregated from thugs and knuckleheads. As he climbed the political ladder to become a two-term President of the United States, he used his bully pulpit to disparage America as unfair, unjust, and racist. While thousands upon thousands of blacks were murdered during his term in office, he focused on the handful of cases involving white police officers who were thrust into hostile situations with tragic results. He consistently portrays blacks as oppressed victims, and demonizes police, a pattern that generates an overwhelming level of animosity among those who believe in his message. This is his legacy.

Here is common sense. A strong nation requires good citizenship. In order to have safe, satisfying, and prosperous communities, we have to foster the right principles. In the media's 24/7 world of talking heads, they propagate a view of the world as being comprised of adversarial dichotomies such as: Democrat/Republican, liberal/conservative, gay/straight, and black/white. Politicians buy into this distorted view. In reality, most people do not like being reduced to such simplistic labels. The proper social focus should be on two critically important continuums (not dichotomies): moral/immoral and prosocial/antisocial. We need common sense notions of right and wrong. Our judgments should be based upon behavior and character – that's a fact.

# AFTERWORD

# RACE AND THE PERSONAL NARRATIVE

Former US Attorney General Eric Holder cried foul when he was pulled over for speeding and the New Jersey state trooper conducted a car check. In recounting this incident, he claimed this was an emblematic of racism and victimization of black males. Somehow, this commonplace event, triggered by his exceeding the speed limit, was deemed important enough to make the national news and give credence to his conspiracy theories. When it comes to dealing with inter-racial situations, I have encountered threats, slurs, attacks, angry mobs, robbery, car theft, and the murder of a friend, all involving blacks. If Holder, Obama, Gates, or Sharpton could tell tales like these involving white folk, publishers would salivate to turn these experiences into a sordid memoir of racism. The media/cultural diversity crowd has no interest in experiences of white people that don't support their socio-political positions.

Everyone has a story, and I find most of them interesting. That is why I became a psychologist. The following are a few personal anecdotes. They are presented to describe the experiences of one white guy. I am neither bragging nor complaining about my past. And, I confess, I am no angel. However, we all evolve, our values take shape, we have choices to make, and we encounter obstacles to be overcome. All of us have encounters that could be described as racist, if that is our goal. At the end of the day, I can confidently say that I am not a racist. I feel no need to apologize for my race or my heritage. I am not the product of privilege. I am a common sense realist.

## PERSONAL NARRATIVE

I grew up in a home with a loving mother and a father who was a role model of hard work, honesty, and courage. He was a part of the Scotch-Irish tradition that would not be bullied or shy away from a fight, and he wanted to instill those qualities in me. He tried to make sure that I would stand up for myself and not shrink from the challenges of life. The following are snippets of my personal journey.

## WHAT I LEARNED ON TORONTO STREET

When I was between four and six years old, we lived in a three-room apartment on a stretch of Toronto Street that runs between Park Avenue and Broad Street, the major north-south thoroughfare in Philadelphia. This is where I learned to socialize with peers. Our block had about fifteen kids (all white). In those days, we were allowed outside, unsupervised, where we played games common to the neighborhood. The boys had a variety of competitive games, including buck-buck, wire ball, step ball, and dodge ball. When we tired of these, we cut a ball in half and played stickball using a sawed-off broom handle as a bat. The girls sometimes enticed us into cooperative games like Red Rover and Simon Says.

Overall, the kids were nice. The exception was Willie, a true bully. He was a tormenter who was about a year older than I. When he abused me, I would go into the house crying. One day, in tears, I grabbed the handle to open the front door and it was locked. The window opened and my father put his head out and said that I could not come into the house crying. Furthermore, he would not let me in until I fought Willie. I was afraid, but felt there was no way around his ultimatum. I put up a tussle, but it was a mismatch that didn't go well for me. This is where my father started giving me lessons on how to hold my own on the street. Lesson number one: *if you are in a fight, hit them first, hit them fast, and hit them as hard as you can.*

During the remainder of the time we lived there, Willie and I had our ups and downs. I mostly developed avoidance techniques. I really didn't want to fight him because he was too much for me to handle. At some level, he terrified me. In fact, after we moved from Toronto Street to 15th Street, I had recurring nightmares that Willie was peering in my bedroom window.

About two years after our move, I ran into Willie while walking through the old neighborhood. He still had an edge, but I was catching up to him in size. Furthermore, I received a Joe Polooka punching bag the previous Christmas. It became my favorite toy. I spent time every day hitting first, fast, and as hard as I could. I was proud of the fact that I could punch Joe's head off and send it flying the length of our living room. As soon as Willie saw me, he started agitating. I hit him with the sequence I had practiced. One punch—fight over—terror exorcized.

Psychologically, this was huge for me. I never had another nightmare involving Willie. My physical self-confidence took a huge step forward. It's not that I never felt fear or intimidation, but I developed a growing courage to stand up for myself. Over time, I developed a reputation for that quality. I wasn't necessarily the best or toughest fighter, but I never backed down. That quality was a double-edged sword. It earned me respect in some cases, and I paid a price in others. I've had stitches, gouged eyes, a broken jaw, and knocked out teeth. But, I learned to stand my ground and never fall prey to bullies. It started on Toronto Street.

## WHAT I LEARNED ON 15TH STREET

We moved from Toronto Street to a bigger apartment on 15th Street when I was six years old; we lived there until I was ten or eleven. This age span covers important formative years for the development of personality and determining the type of adult a child becomes. This period in my life was rich in learning opportunities. The following are some of the most important lessons.

**Lesson One: Be Self-reliant and Resilient**. Our apartment on Toronto Street was small and the street itself was the width of an alley. We moved to a larger apartment on 15th Street near Westmoreland Avenue. Although Kenderton Elementary School was at the end of our block, I was allowed to continue in the school where I started, Simon Muhr at Germantown and Allegheny Avenues. The primary reason for my parents keeping me at Muhr was the racial makeup of the schools. Kenderton had a high percentage of blacks, while Muhr was 100 percent white. Attending Muhr meant walking seven blocks to school instead of one block, but I did what I was told.

My father drove me to school the day after our move. I went through the day, and, at dismissal time, left the building and stepped onto the sidewalk. With a bolt of shock, I realized that I didn't know how to get home. I had never walked from Germantown and Allegheny to 15th and Westmoreland. I fretted over what to do. We were a very blue-collar family in which my father and most all of my aunts and uncles left school after eighth grade to find jobs and support the family during the Great Depression. (Bernie, whites do understand what it means to be poor.) To me, teachers were a dramatically different breed in the way they looked, spoke, and acted. At age six, I literally thought they went into a state of suspended animation at the end of the day, then waited for the children to return the next morning. Holding that belief, I felt there was no sense re-entering the building for help.

I struggled to control my angst and weigh my options. Looking across the intersection, I saw Jimmy Doyle's Sinclair service station. I knew Jimmy would call my dad if I went to the station; however, the intersection I needed to cross was convoluted and intimidating, with a confluence of three busy streets—Germantown, Allegheny, and Sedgley Avenues-that had a great deal of traffic and trolley cars running in two directions. I felt most comfortable walking back to Toronto Street. From there I knew how to get to Frunzi's Café, the corner bar where my father drank and where I knew the owner and all the regular patrons. So, I walked to my old block, crossed Broad Street for the first time on my own, and went up Indiana Avenue to Frunzi's.

When I entered the bar, I told Herman the owner/bartender my plight. I lamented, "My mom and dad moved, and they didn't tell me where they lived." He did what good bartenders do and asked, "Do you want a drink?" I ordered a coke. Because I knew taproom protocol at an early age, I reached in my pocket, pulled out a dollar my father had given me that morning, and put it on the bar. Tommy James was seated next to me. He laughed and asked if I'd buy him a drink. I agreed, and Tommy ordered a beer (10 cents for drafts). John Gallagher was next to Tommy and asked if I would buy him a drink. I said, "Okay," and he ordered a shot and a beer. Now, I knew the dollar was going fast. Then, Tommy pushed me over the edge by asking if I'd buy a round for the bar. At that point, I burst into tears, ran out the door, sat on the ladies entrance steps, and refused to come inside. When my parents arrived, I wouldn't enter the bar area because I was still furious with Tommy. My mother and Nat Frunzi, Herman's wife who ran the café's outstanding kitchen, lured me into the dining room with a meatball sandwich and settled me down.

Despite this trauma, Frunzi's remained one of my favorite spots. We spent at least one night per week going there as a family. The place fascinated me and was a sensory and social wonderland with the smell of stale beer, the blue haze of cigarette smoke, the frequent hacking of "smoker's cough," bar stool seats that spun on steel ball bearings, the shuffle board, the dart board, a juke box where I was allowed to pick six songs for a quarter, Herman's thirty-two caliber hammerless pistol that rested under the far end of the bar, and cab drivers coming in with wild stories of misadventure with their fares. I loved it. The place had great food, a lot of people who liked me, and a steady stream of interesting action. It was stimulating and educational, teaching me worldly lessons at an early age. With guys like Tommy, it also helped me develop a thick skin and learn to take a joke.

**Lesson Two: Urban Blight.** After the first-day trauma getting home from school, I quickly gained my bearings. I learned the route to school. Frunzi's was a six-block jaunt down 15th Street. If you passed Frunzi's, crossed Indiana Avenue and walked through North Philadelphia Train Station, you reached Glenwood

Avenue and Rush Street where my grandparents, aunts, and uncles lived. So, I traveled 15th Street on a regular basis. It also was a short walk to my father's garage, Mike's Auto Repair, at 17th and Allegheny where I began doing odd jobs as a six year old.

The neighborhood was changing during the 1950s. Steadily, more blacks moved in. Listening to adults at Frunzi's explain the situation, they said these newcomers were *Blockbusters* being brought up from the South by Democrats who were trying to increase their voting constituency. As the neighborhood transformed, its general appearance changed in ways more substantial than the color of people's skin. Very quickly, property began to deteriorate. One particular house struck me because the front door often stood ajar and I could see inside. These row homes had small vestibules with a flight of stairs leading to the second floor. In this home, every other stair tread was missing. When I asked my father what was going on, he said the people living there tore out the wooden treads and burned them as firewood. These homes all had furnaces and coal bins in the basement. These new neighbors wanted kindling. Their solution—burn their stair treads.

In a neighborhood that had been known for people who not only cleaned inside their houses but also scrubbed their stoops and sidewalks, these newcomers chose to destroy their home tread by tread. Even as a kid, I knew this was stupid. Although the term may not have been popular at the time, "urban blight" did not appear to be a condition that swallowed deserving folks. It looked like a condition created by people who made bad choices. Scrubbing your stoop is a choice. Burning your stair treads is a choice. The impact on the climate of a neighborhood is profound.

**Lesson Three: The Behavior of Crabs in a Basket**. An enduring figure from my walks down 15th Street was an old man who used to sit on his front steps. His skin was coal black, his tongue and the palms of his hands were vivid pink, his eyes were bloodshot, and his voice was gravely with a southern accent. He was totally exotic to me and a little scary, but we struck up a passing friendship. He never failed to engage me with a look, nod, or casual conversation. He also appealed to my fascination with knives, because he was always whittling.

One day, when I was about eight years old, he stopped me and posed a question. He looked serious and his intensity hit my alert button. He asked: "Do you know why my people will never get ahead?" This took me off guard. The concepts of "my people" and "getting ahead" were new to me. These socio-political phenomena were beyond my third-grade wheelhouse. When I responded "No," he explained: "My people are like crabs in a basket. Do you know what happens with crabs in a basket?" Again, a meek "No" from me. He elaborated,

"When crabs are in a basket, if one tries to get out do you know what the other crabs do?" A third consecutive "No." "They pull it right back down. No crab gets out of that basket because the others won't let that happen. They pull each other back, hold each other down, and none of them get free."

His sincerity and depth of feeling struck a chord in the emotional center of my brain. I found the concept sad and painful. The visual image of the basket and crabs made an impression that remains vivid. It's a thought that lingers with me today when I hear accounts of "his people" in this type of neighborhood. Endless rounds of drugs, crime, chaotic schools, and violence —burned out and boarded up houses, scant commercial enterprise—the end-products of crabs in a basket. This sorry state originates with bad choices that cause frustration, misery, and devastation. Charles Barkley believes it. I heard that Frederick Douglass did too.

**Lesson Four: It's Not Easy to Succeed in the 'Hood.** Beyond the regulars, there were numerous individuals who frequented Frunzi's. Among those that I found most interesting were the Catholic priest, the numbers runner, and the shoe shine boy. The priest was an alcoholic who came periodically for a free drink. Since the neighborhood had a plethora of corner bars, he could catch quite a load by getting just one free drink at each stop, heading in a different direction each day. I found that kind of pathetic. Gambling was popular, and the numbers runner came every day to pick up the numbers and horse race bets booked by Herman. There was a mystique and excitement to rubbing shoulders with a representative of the Mafia. Guys would talk about things that happened to those who crossed the Mob and didn't pay their debts. I learned terms such as curbing, where the individual's mouth was placed against the curb and his head stomped, knocking out his teeth. Then there was knee capping where the person's leg was placed over the curb and stomped, breaking the knee. I cringed at the thought of these activities.

Another favorite was the shoeshine boy, Reecie, a black kid slightly older than me. My dad loved Reecie. He was funny, charismatic, and talented. As he worked, I would watch him open the can of polish, dip in with his fingertips, smear the wax on the shoes, and then buff them, using his buffing rag like a percussion instrument with the popping and snapping. In my view, he had enviable talent. I emulated his style whenever I shined my own shoes.

With Frunzie's being next to the train station, travelers from all over stopped in for a drink or a meal as they waited to make connections. One night a guy with a southern accent ordered a shine. When Reecie finished, the guy refused to pay, saying, "I'm not going to pay that nigger boy." My father had a temper and this guy provoked it. He told the guy to pay; the guy told my dad to mind his own business. Bad choice. My dad punched him and sent him sprawling across the floor. Reecie got his quarter, and a tip.

Part of what my father loved about Reecie was how hard he worked, a trait my father held as a clear virtue. Race didn't matter; it was the character of the individual, and Reecie had a good one. However, as the neighborhood changed, it wasn't easy to run a business, even as a shoeshine boy working for a quarter per shine. Survival strategies became essential. Every time Reecie had four quarters, he asked Herman to exchange them for a dollar. He carefully folded the bill and placed it in his hatband to hide it from the growing number of thugs on the street who tried to shake him down. I thought this was sad. Reecie was a good kid who was trying to make something for himself and maybe for his family. The crabs were after him. I hope he made it out.

**Lesson Five: When Enough is Enough**. The neighborhood's demographic change was surging by 1955 when I was ten years old, and the quality of life eroding quickly. You had to be more careful of where you walked. As a white kid, it was hard to pass through some areas without being accosted. It started to feel like my name was, "Gimme a quarter, man." To handle yourself in this environment, you had to practice your lines, style, and delivery. First, show no fear. Second, have your line ready. My typical verbal response was the grammatically poor double negative, "I ain't got no quarter" or the more profanely emphasized version, "I ain't got no f*ckin' quarter." Third, use your body language. I was taught to put a hand in one pocket to give the impression I was reaching for a weapon. It didn't matter if you had a weapon, just put the thought in their minds. By watching where I went and using these strategies, I never gave up a quarter.

My record came to an end one night in the North Philadelphia Railroad Station driveway. We were at Frunzi's and another boy and I told our parents that we were heading to the station to watch the crowd. The station was fascinating with its schedules, announcements, and stream of passengers. If you were a people watcher, it was a fun place to visit. There were special times, such as when the circus came to town, when the place became spectacular.

As we walked down the drive, six black boys emerged from behind a hedge and surrounded us. One of them stuck a knife in my back and they told us to give them our money. I thought about fighting, but I could feel the point of the knife, looked at the odds, and believed discretion was the better part of valor. They got some pocket change from us. When they left, we returned to Frunzi's and I told my father what happened. His temper flared immediately, and he told me to come with him. We walked across the street to a corner store that sold candy. The kids that robbed us were there spending my money. I pointed to the one with the knife and another who did a good bit of threatening. Dad grabbed them by their collars, pulled them across the street to Frunzi's, and told Herman to call the police.

I have no idea how the word spread so quickly, but a crowd started gathering immediately. The only other white person outside was Dad's friend, Russell. The growing mob of blacks people was yelling, threatening, and calling out racial slurs. Black women hung out second-story windows shouting down into the street. I looked around the bar to see who was going to help my dad—no one. Herman was on the phone with the police and laid his hammerless 32 caliber pistol on the bar in case the mob entered. One of the regulars panicked and retreated to the dining room. I couldn't stand the thought of my father being in danger because of something that started with me, so I ran out to help. My exit was so fast that my mother didn't have time to stop me.

Dad and Russell stood with their backs to the wall so they couldn't be jumped from behind. Even in 1955, my father had a carry permit and always had a revolver tucked under his shirt. I knew he would use it if things turned ugly. I stood near dad, facing the crowd. Kids in the group immediately came my way, getting in my face with threats and racial slurs. Then, I heard punches landing as Russell and one of the black men went at it. About that time, several police cars rolled up because Herman told them a "race riot" was in progress. The police settled things down and took the two boys into custody.

My father was attentive to detail. He made sure that he knew the boys' names. Since Russell lived on the same block as these robbers, he provided my father with updates. The boy with the knife was probably a year older than me when this happened. He continued to get into trouble, eventually making the newspaper when he was arrested for murder.

This robbery was the straw that broke the camel's back. We moved to the predominantly white northeast section of Philadelphia later that year. The popular term is *white flight*. The sad fact is that no reasonable person wants to live in an environment where you can't let your children walk down the street without placing them at risk. Such social situations are deplorable. My father and his seven siblings were born in the house on Rush Street. His business was blocks away. Patrons at Frunzi's Café continued to insist this change was the Democratic Party's effort to increase their constituency. There was no evidence of white privilege in this setting. A core of antisocialists ruined it for everyone.

Bernie Sanders opined, "When you are white, you don't know what it's like to be living in a ghetto, you don't know what it's like to be poor, you don't know what it's like to be hassled when you are walking down a street or dragged out of a car." Bernie Sanders doesn't have a clue.

## THE DOYLES

The Doyles lived near us on Mayfield Street. This Irish-Catholic family had ten children. My father had been friends with them since childhood and began working for Mr. Doyle, who owned the first towing businesses (started in 1915) in Philadelphia, as a teenager. Mr. Doyle was a piece of work. My favorite story about him was the day that he was in a bar, got very drunk, and became overly rambunctious. The bartender flagged him and told him to leave. Mr. Doyle, displeased with the situation, went out, backed his tow truck to the front door, dragged in the cable and tow hook, and attached the hook to the bar. He was going to drag the bar into the street. If he couldn't drink, no one would drink. They managed to usher both him and his hook out of the place. Crazy but harmless.

The Doyles always had a special place in our life. Ro was my mother's best friend. My dad travelled with the boys. I was named after Jerry Doyle, the second youngest of the clan. Jerry was a sweet kid and a favorite of my dad's. Unfortunately, he died of pancreatic cancer when he was six years old. Although Jerry was gone before I was born, I believe my relationship with him goes beyond being a namesake. A fortune-telling gypsy on the Wildwood, New Jersey, boardwalk hypothesized the nature of our relationship. One evening, we stopped to have our fortunes told. When the gypsy came to me, she said that she saw a guardian angel watching over me. The angel she described matched Jerry Doyle. It may seem weird, but there are times in my life that I absolutely felt protected by a guardian angel. I have always believed that angel was Jerry.

The Doyles suffered losses. After Jerry's death, his younger brother, Larry, was struck and killed by a truck on Germantown Avenue. Then, Mrs. and Mr. Doyle died within a six-month span. Possibly because of all this loss, Tommy and Johnny Doyle struggled with mental health demons. At different points they were in psychiatric care, as well as being homeless. It was tough, because at their best they were terrific people. Tommy was one of the funniest men I have ever known. He could literally make me fall out of my chair laughing at his wildly animated stories about driving trucks across country. Johnny had a sweet and gentle personality.

Johnny met an unfortunate end. I got details from one of Tommy's friends. He said that Johnny and Tommy were around a McDonald's near Roosevelt Boulevard and Adams Avenue when a large black man whose nickname was "Big" something or other accosted them. He threw Johnny to the ground, smashing his skull. Tommy ran from the scene and ended up miles away at his sister's house. When he arrived, he told them what happened but did not want the police called for fear this killer would come after the family. Apparently, this animal was well known and extremely vicious. This was an interracial murder gone unpublicized and unpunished. No outcry of "white lives matter." No witnesses to testify. A life lost for no good reason.

## EARLY ONSET

As a behavior management specialist, I conducted many classroom observations. Those that I found most toubling involved students with oppositonal and defiant mindsets. Many of these students had good potential, but it was negated by their attitude. This too often involved Blacks. In one case, I was asked to observe the behavior of a first grader. During a 75-minute observation, I saw a well-prepared lesson about making bread. The teacher had organized a combination of illustrations, discussion, and hands-on activities that culminated with students tasting different types of bread and describing their favorite. Most students were interested, cooperative, and involved; this boy was not. He was rude and aggressive toward classmates and defiant when the teacher tried to engage him. Listed below are some of his comments.

"I don't care."

"You can't make me."

"My mother will punch you in the face."

"I don't have to listen to you."

"I ain't doing this."

"I can get rid of teachers."

"I'll hit (him). I'll hit him in the head."

"I love to hit (her)."

"Who cares?"

"You're history." (to the teacher)

*"Shut your mouth!" (to the teacher)*

This is the kind of disruption that Dawn Baldesi, the Normandy High School teacher, referred to when she stated, "Teaching is very difficult. Teachers get cussed out, yelled at. There are so many write-ups you can't keep up." Exacerbating the problem with this child was the fact that his mother gave the school no support. In fact, she went into attack mode whenever she received a call from school. She was a nasty piece of cheese. She modeled and reinforced her son's hostile and self-defeating behavior and attitude, pointing him toward disaster.

## VIETNAM

The majority of my first two years in the Army was spent in training. My assignments included basic training, advanced training, and a stint working in the personnel section of 1ˢᵗ Armored Division at Fort Hood, Texas. I quickly decided that clerk-typing wasn't for me. I took the Army language test, did well, then began a full year of Vietnamese language school in El Paso, Texas. This was followed by a month of psychological operations training at Fort Bragg's Special Warfare School. I left for Vietnam in September 1968.

The flight to Vietnam was interesting. Troops from all over the country came to San Francisco where we boarded a TWA plane and headed out. Although ages seemed to range from 18 to 45, the vast majority of troops were younger than 21. Each of us handled our thoughts and apprehensions in our own way – loud, quiet, rambunctious, sleepy – whatever worked. We had a two-hour layover in Hawaii as the plane refueled. Many of the young guys re-boarded with fifths of bourbon, intent on partying through the rest of the flight. Because I was older, I had no interest in booze. I accepted a drink or two for the sake of sociability but wanted to be sober when my boots hit the ground.

The pilot informed us when we gained sight of Vietnam. Looking out the window, I got the big-game butterflies. There was no predicting what the year would bring. We landed at Tan Son Nhat Airport, filed down the steps, and lined up on a tarmac that seemed as hot as a frying pan. Waves of heat hit me in the face and the sun pounded down. Noncommissioned officers shouted orders. I don't know how long their harangue lasted, but as we stood in formation the young drunks started feeling the heat. One after another they began projectile vomiting across the sweltering ground. My tour had begun.

I headed to the 4ᵗʰ Psychological Operations Group in Saigon where I was interviewed and given my assignment. They told me that I would lead a ground broadcast team for the 7ᵗʰ Psychological Battalion in support of First Marine Division. Say what? Serving my year with the Marines? I didn't see that one coming either.

My initial work was with the 7th Marine Regiment on Hill 55 where I received a quick on-the-job orientation from the Marine I was replacing, Joe Geng. Joe was a hard charger from north New Jersey who approached psychological operations with a grunt's mentality. In fact, Joe was a gung-ho grunt, winning a Bronze Star for his role in helping a recon unit shoot their way out of North Vietnamese ambush.

During the brief time we had together, I never felt fully comfortable riding with him. Part of this was because there was a bullet hole through the passenger side of the windshield where I sat. When we set up to broadcast, there were bullet holes through the speaker. These seemed like ominous signs of things to come. Joe taught me approaches never mentioned during my Fort Bragg training. His favorite technique was "harassment broadcasting." In this approach, if the Viet Cong (VC) or North Vietnamese Army (NVA) shoot at you with small arms fire, let them know that they will receive artillery fire in return. If they fire mortars, inform them that bombs are on the way. If the enemy keeps firing, never shut up, never back down, always let them know that fire and brimstone are on the way. Joe was a piece of work. He taught me a lot in a short time.

There are three important things to know about leading a ground broadcast team. First, you have to get close enough to the enemy so they can hear you. Second, they always know exactly where you are because you are blaring at them through a loudspeaker. Third, keep your speaker high and your head low.

I transferred to support the 5th Marine Regiment in the An Hoa Basin in December, 1968. I already knew some guys with 5th Marines from supporting them during a joint operation. An Hoa was a bloody place where many good men died on both sides. Located 25 miles southwest of DaNang, the area was among the most heavily contested in Vietnam. It wasn't far from the Ho Chi Minh Trail. An NVA infantry division occupied the low-lying mountains to the west. The basin itself had battalions of Viet Cong. There was no safe place when you served with 5th Marine Regiment.

The typical Marine grunt spent at least 75 percent of his time in the bush where he was subject to attack and booby traps at every juncture. Mortar and rocket attacks on the Regimental base were common. Casualty rates were high. Virginia Senator and presidential candidate Jim Webb wrote about his experience with in the An Hoa Basin, noting that officers in rifle companies had an 85 percent chance of being killed or wounded. (Because our tour dates overlapped, I'm sure that Webb and I worked together at some point.) Companies earned names such as "Dying Delta." In addition to enemy fire, ongoing exposure to the elements and bad water resulted in assorted ailments. Senator Webb concluded his article with the following sentiment:

Like every military unit throughout history we had occasional laggards, cowards, and complainers. But in the aggregate these Marines were the finest people I have ever been around. It has been my privilege to keep up with many of them over the years since we all came home. One finds in them very little bitterness about the war in which they fought. The most common regret, almost to a man, is that they were not able to do more—for each other and for the people they came to help.

It would be redundant to say that I would trust my life to these men, because I already have in more ways than I can ever recount. I am alive today because of their quiet, unaffected heroism. Such valor epitomizes the conduct of Americans at war from the first days of our existence. That the boomer elites can canonize this sort of conduct in our fathers' generation while ignoring it in our own is more than simple oversight. It is a conscious, continuing travesty. [1]

I worked with 5th Marines' S-5 Civil Affairs Unit. S-5 had the responsibility of serving as liaison between the military and civilian population. The Army recruiting website notes that working in S-5 "combines regional expertise, language competency, political-military awareness, cross-cultural communication and professional military skills to conduct civil affairs operations and support civilian-military operations in support of conventional and special operations forces." Yep, that's what we did. This was cross-cultural competency in action.

**Lieutenant Henehan**. Henehan was in charge of S-5 for most of the time I spent with 5th Marines. He was yet *another* north Jersey guy. Two specific incidents capture the kind of person and leader he was.

The first incident began on February 23, 1969, when incoming mortar and rocket fire hit An Hoa Combat Base's ammunition dump. As we sat in our fighting holes on the base perimeter, tremendous explosions boomed throughout the night. All sorts of munitions were either detonated or catapulted through the air and strewn into the surrounding rice paddies. Within days, the VC and NVA booby trapped these munitions, killing and wounding Marines. One of my team's jobs was broadcasting reward messages, informing villagers that they would be paid if they turned in booby traps or live munitions. We were not having much success, and another Marine rifle squad was taken out with a booby trapped 155mm artillery round, killing a good friend of Henehan's. He sprang into action.

We went into Duc Duc Refugee Hamlet and did some quick research. We found that villagers were being paid for returned munitions with IOUs and the redemption process was slow to nonexistent. Those who were paid received less than the amount specified on the posters we distributed. The program's credibility was in the toilet.

Henehan quickly obtained cash to pay rewards and we returned to the hamlet. Because of my Vietnamese language skills, I was well known and tended to draw a crowd of kids whenever I showed up. We told the villagers that we would pay them on the spot for any ordinance brought to us. No one seemed impressed since they had been stiffed before. This is what set Henehan apart. He wanted results. He wanted them quickly. He wanted to restore credibility and save the lives and limbs of Marines and civilians. We took matters into our own hands.

We talked with a group of kids and asked them to help us find 155mm artillery rounds in the rice paddies. They had no trouble leading us to what we wanted. We jumped into the paddy, dug out four rounds with our entrenching tools, and laid the rounds on the dyke. Each round weighs 97 pounds. Henehan lashed a round on a pole so that he and one of the kids could carry it back to the village where a truck was waiting to load ordinance. My partner, Ray White, and another Vietnamese kid did the same thing. I decided to show off and lifted a round onto my shoulder to carry it back myself. A Vietnamese teenager saw this and quickly asked his friends to lift the remaining round onto his shoulder. Once it was in place, he looked at me and smiled. The race was on.

Vietnamese know how to carry things. They do a little shuffle, bouncing under the burden while they glide along. They never seem to bear the full weight. I, on the other hand, was a lumbering Yankee. I was bigger but plodding and inefficient when compared with the competition. It was probably 3/8 of a mile back to the truck. The crowd grew as the kid and I raced along the dyke and through the hamlet. Kids cheered as they ran beside of us. Women with betel nut-coated teeth smiled. My shoulder was killing me. I periodically rolled the shell around my neck to switch shoulders. I was in agony and it took every ounce of strength, but I beat the kid by one step. Exhausted, I leaned over and let the shell slide off my shoulder and fall to the ground. You might not believe that it's possible to think two complete sentences in the split second it takes a heavy object to fall from shoulder height to the ground, but my mind screamed: "You dumb ass! That's an artillery round!" I heard a "thunk." Thank God! Henehan and Ray rolled in with their partners and the kids were paid on the spot. Watching this, the villagers were off to the races.

I was required to submit activity reports to Headquarters on a regular basis. My report dated April 20, 1969, included the following information:

The following items were turned in between the dates of March 23 and April 18:

| | |
|---|---|
| 225 | 155 mm projectiles |
| 797 | 105 mm projectiles |
| 1,064 | 81 mm mortar rounds |
| 875 | 60 mm mortar rounds |
| 1 | 175 mm projectile |
| 3 | 8 inch projectiles |
| 18 | 106 mm rounds |
| 117 | Bouncing Betty mines |
| 42 | 4.2 inch mortar rounds |
| 2 | 250 pound bombs |
| 1 | 140 mm rocket |
| 6 | Rifle grenades |
| 18 | Chi com grenades |
| 5 | M79 rounds |
| 4 | M26 grenades |
| 3 | Claymore mines |
| 1 | Block TNT |
| 3 | Satchel charges |
| 5 | AK47 magazines with rounds |

Each of those items represented potential death and destruction. Henehan led the way in getting them to where they would do no harm.

A second interesting Henehan story involved our houseboy. S-5 managed the Vietnamese who worked on base. Most of them spent their days filling sandbags that were used to fortify areas around the base, including living quarters. S-5 would process the workers at the beginning and end of each day. We had several favorites that included Tram Bam, the crew chief, and three kids, John Henry, Murph the Surf, and Charlie Brown, who served as our houseboys. Tram Bam was an amazing guy. He was thin as a rail and looked 65 years old. Despite his slight build and wrinkled appearance, he was tough as nails. He outworked guys half his age, and he ran a tight ship.

Competition is the normal order of things when you put a bunch of guys together. We had a pull-up bar next to our office and would compete. Sergeant Boehm was the best we had. He could have been the model for a Marine Corps recruiting poster. He was fit, muscular, and handsome. One day we were having a contest and I managed about 15 pull-ups. Boehm jumped on and easily beat me with 22 reps. Tram Bam watched then asked if he could get in the contest. We laughed and had to lift him up to the bar. He easily completed 25 then dropped to the ground with a smile. What a guy!

The houseboys didn't do much work, but they were funny and their modest remuneration helped support their families. One day, John Henry didn't show up for work. We found out that Duc Duc District Police arrested him because he refused to give up part of his pay when they tried to shake him down. Henehan went through channels trying to get John Henry released but had no luck. When word got back that John Henry was being abused, Henehan went off.

Three interesting weapons hung on our wall. There were AK47 and S5 rifles captured in combat, and a vintage World War II grease gun. Henehan grabbed the grease gun then locked and loaded. He told Sergeant Schaf and me to grab our M16s, because we were going to get John Henry. I wasn't sure this was a good idea and felt totally uncertain that it was going to end well. I hated to think that I would meet my end in a shootout with the Duc Duc police. We jumped in the jeep and headed to their District Headquarters. Henehan sped into the courtyard and slammed on the brakes. He jumped out, sprayed a few rounds in the air, yelling that he wanted John Henry. Schaf and I had our M16s ready as we waited to see who would emerge.

My team sometimes broadcasted from Duc Duc Headquarters because this facility sat on a hill facing directly into hostile territory. Our speakers carried well from there during nighttime broadcasts. The district police liked me and were overly flattering about my Vietnamese language proficiency. When we talked, they always got in my personal space, putting their hands on my legs and petting the hair on my arms, a physical attribute that seemed to fascinate them. This was all part of winning the hearts and mind.

Maybe because they saw me, they sent representatives to speak with us. They refused to release John Henry, and Henehan, with his 12-week training in Vietnamese, tried to make his point in a very emotional manner. Being somewhat more fluent in the language, I assured those in charge that trung-uy dien ca dau (Lieutenant Crazy in the Head) wasn't leaving without our houseboy. I pleaded and cajoled, Henehan stood his ground with the grease gun, and we eventually secured John Henry's release. Henehan was reported to the Regimental commander and came extremely close to being court martialed.

**Ray White**. Our three-man ground broadcast team was as multicultural as it gets. I was the team leader, my Army partner was Ray White (black), and our native interpreter was Tran Viet Minh (Vietnamese). Ray was everything you could want in a partner. A salt of the earth guy who was very laid back and wanted nothing more than to return home and marry his girlfriend whom he loved dearly. Her letters were like treasures when they arrived. During relaxing times, he liked to play the guitar and gave heartfelt renditions of Smokey Robinson's *Tracks of My Tears*. In the field, he was a terrific. He never flinched in difficult situations. He held up under the stress that humping with Marine's in the bush can impose such as nighttime maneuvers through rice paddies, going for extended periods without being resupplied with food or water, carrying a 60 pounds of equipment and supplies, broadcasting through a barrage of enemy fire, and, sleeping in muck. Ray was always there, always reliable, and always a friend. We three came from different backgrounds but worked as a team. If only one of us had water, we passed the canteen. If someone ran out of food, we shared. Race was the last thing on our minds. We shared a common goal - surviving – together. I think this is the way that most of us operate.

While we had no difficulty getting along and dealing with tough situations, the "real world" had troubles of its own. We heard news of protests, riots, organized groups intent on bring down the "establishment," and all kinds of "black power" chatter. These seemed like tales of anarchists. Shootouts with police, armed confrontations, burning of neighborhoods - this was sickening.

The Black Power fist was present even among Marines in the An Hoa Basin. I never liked it, believing that it was a racist sign. If we drove by Blacks and they saw Ray in the truck, they would raise the fist. I'd look at Ray to see his response, which was usually a sheepish raised fist in return. I asked him if he considered this black power movement to be racist, and if he went along with the hostility often associated with it. His responses tended to be equivocal. He seemed caught in the middle. On one level, he seemed embarrassed. He was the only Black in S-5 and one of the few in our psychological operations battalion. Wherever we went, Ray was just one of the guys. We all got along and treated each other with respect. We liked one another. Race was never an issue. At the same time, Ray felt pressure to demonstrate loyalty to the "brothers." Not an easy spot for him.

The only real clash that I witnessed between Blacks and Whites once again occurred the mess hall. A group of blacks butted in the front of the line "to be with their home boys." A white Marine said something and they jumped him, punching him in the head several times. I was in the back of the line and not near the action and the assault ended quickly. Those close to the victim never intervened.

**A Difficult Day**. The saying goes that *war is hell and battle is a motherf*cker.* Anybody who has served in combat knows that you can never predict what will happen from one moment to the next. One day we crossed into Arizona Territory, a hotbed of enemy activity across the river from our base, to participate in a "County Fair." The primary mission was clearing out civilians remaining in the area who were caught in the crossfire between the NVA and Marines. The civilians would be relocated to the refugee hamlet, and any structures, trenches, or spider holes that could be useful to the enemy would be destroyed. Because I would be a key figure in talking with civilians, I chose not go in full battle gear. I left my steel pot, flak jacket, and M16 behind, traveling in my bush cap, fatigues, and carrying my 45 caliber pistol and K-Bar knife as weapons. My reasoning was that the day would involve a lot of face-to-face contact, and I wanted the Vietnamese to feel comfortable.

We crossed the river and weren't very far into the day when the action started. The area was full of NVA. I was walking along a rice paddy dyke with a rifle squad when we came under fire. Probably because I stood out as vulnerable with no steel pot or flak jacket, I seemed to be a primary target during the initial burst of enemy fire. Several bullets whizzed past me, one coming so close to my head that I felt the breeze and heard a snap as it went by. I jumped into the paddy, returning fire with my 45 at targets I couldn't see. Very quickly, artillery fire, then bombs were called in on the tree line.

We emerged from the muck and headed toward a tree line. The Marine walking point no sooner reached the tree line when he was shot. As I ducked down a guy shouted, "Marine down. Help me get him out of here." This was one of those emotionally charged moments of choice. Thoughts and rationalizations spun through my mind such as: "Someone has just been shot and the shooter is still in place and aiming this way;" "I'm not a Marine, I'm in the Army;" "I'm here to do psychological operations, not to be a grunt;" "I'm too vulnerable because I'm not wearing a steel pot of flak jacket;" and, most importantly, "I'd like to live and get home." Because I worked with different companies on every assignment, I didn't know most of these guys beyond passing contact.

This is where values and will power are tested. An American Marine was in trouble and needed help. It was possible that a minute's delay could be the difference between life and death. I jumped up and got to him as quickly as possible. The other Marine and I grabbed him by the flak jacket and dragged him out of harm's way. There was no multicultural thought regarding race. The essential thing was that he was a Marine and he needed help.

When I finally looked, he was dead. A handsome kid who was about 19 years old. He took a single bullet through the heart. This was the face of sacrifice.

The Marine motto is Semper Fi, always faithful. This young man laid his life on the line for the values of duty, honor, and country. My response wasn't an act of heroism. It was a commitment to values and the exertion of free will to follow those values. In any war, there are countless examples of such commitment.

**Surprised and Honored**. As I processed out of Vietnam, an officer at Group headquarters in Saigon called me into his office. He informed me that I was being awarded a Bronze Star and read the citation to me. I was moved. This was unexpected. The medal and citation sat in a drawer for decades before my wife talked me into framing it and hanging it in my office. I am now 71 years old, a cancer survivor, and possibly waxing nostalgic. The citation seems more important to me now, possibly because it acknowledges the manner in which I have tried to live my life. It reads:

> *By direction of the President, the Bronze Star Medal is presented to Specialist Five Gerald M. McMullen, U.S. Army, who distinguished himself by outstandingly meritorious service in connection with military operations against a hostile force in the Republic of Vietnam. During the period October 1968 to July 1969 he consistently manifested exemplary professionalism and initiative in obtaining outstanding results. His rapid assessment and solution of numerous problems inherent in a combat environment greatly enhanced the allied effectiveness against a determined and aggressive enemy. Despite many adversities, he invariable performed his duties in a resolute and efficient manner. Energetically applying his sound judgment and extensive knowledge, he has contributed materially to the successful accomplishment of the United States mission in the Republic of Vietnam. His loyalty, diligence and devotion to duty were in keeping with the highest traditions of the military service and reflect great credit upon himself and the United States Army.*

Loyalty, diligence, and devotion to duty are values that I've tried to use as guideposts in my life. Problem solving has been and always will be a strong motivating factor for me. My father taught me the importance of standing strong in the face of aggressive adversaries. Seeing these qualities recognized and appreciated seem to mean more to me now.

**Postscript**: I googled An Hoa Combat Base and Duc Duc Resettlement Hamlet and uncovered disturbing information. Sadly, I found an entry by Alan Waugh titled *The Duc Duc Resettlement Village Massacre.*[2] He reported that on the morning of March 29, 1971, two North Vietnamese Army battalions along with Viet Cong sappers entered Duc Duc, burning the hamlet to the ground (1,500 homes were destroyed) and killing or wounding hundreds of men, women, and children. The crime committed by these civilians was supporting Americans in the An Hoa Valley. I had not known about this incident. My heart breaks when I think about it.

## A LAST LOOK AT OBAMA

Seeds sown by Barack Obama are tragically coming to fruition during 2016, his eighth year in office. His relentless anti-police mantra has yielded bloody results as mentally unstable black individuals set out to kill white police officers and the Niggaz wit Attitude musical rap group, "f**k the police" chant reverberates through black neighborhoods. In Dallas, Micah Xavier Johnson declared that he wanted to "kill white people, especially police officers." He assassinated Lorne Ahrens, Michael Krol, Michael J. Smith, Brent Thompson, and Patrick Zamarripa, and wounded eleven other people. Obama was at a meeting in Spain when news of this event broke. Part of his response included:

> "There are legitimate issues that have been raised, and there's data and evidence to back up the concerns that are being expressed by these protesters.... And if police organizations and departments acknowledge that there's a problem and there's an issue, then that, too, is going to contribute to real solutions. And, as I said yesterday, that is what's going to ultimately help make the job of being a cop a lot safer." [3]

So, cops still act stupidly in his view, and it can be inferred that Johnson is the victim of injustice. That presidential stance hasn't changed. Obama has tried to engrain that view into the minds of Americans and the world. Days after this speech, Gavin Eugene Long, who railed against "crackers," Arabs, and Chinese, assassinated officers Matthew Gerald, Brad Garafola, and Montrell L. Jackson in Baton Rouge, Louisiana. Jackson, who was black, expressed the anguish of being a police officer in the current atmosphere, describing himself as "tired physically and emotionally." Just as we see in education, when disruptors grind on the system without accountability, it becomes bail out or burn out for those trying to bring respect and responsibility to antisocial situations. Days before his assassination, this good man wrote, "I swear to God I love this city but I wonder if this city loves me. In uniform I get nasty hateful looks and out of uniform some consider me a threat." [4]

Jessica Chasmar's July 18, 2016, article in The Washington Times,[5] presents the views of Milwaukee County Sheriff David Clarke, a black law enforcement officer whose speech at the Republican National Convention went largely unrecognized by the mainstream media. Prior to the convention, Clarke described these recent assassinations as "guerrilla urban warfare" against police, the Constitution and American ideals. He said the police killings represented "…a civil war unfolding within our borders." He lays the blame for these antisocial tragedies at the feet of Barack Obama and the Black Lives Matter movement that he has encouraged, endorsed, and invited to the White House for counsel. Clarke states that "Black Lives Matter organizers hold the same values of America's age-old enemies, who have always fought the ideals of our Constitution and our nation. That they have now taken on as their costume a false concern for Black America only adds to their depravity." When it comes to Obama, Clarke explains, "The disgust and contempt I have for this president's and his party's actions could not be more complete."

And, in the city where Obama extols his accomplishments as a community organizer, the July 18, 2016, edition of the Chicago Tribune informs us that the number of citizens shot is nearly 2,200 and the death toll has reached 329, about 100 more than the number of murders recorded at this time in 2015.[5]

# END NOTES

**Acknowledgement**: I would like to preface my references by expressing my gratitude to *Wikipedia*. I made extensive use of this well-conceived resource when doing background research, employing it to gain an overview of almost every person, place, and thing mentioned in this book. It was tremendously helpful.

## CHAPTER 1
1. Alex Griswold, "Bernie Sanders to Liberty U.: America Was Founded on 'Racist Principles'," *Mediate*, September 14, 2015.
2. Louis P Pojman, *Ethics: Discovering Right and Wrong* (Belmont, CA: Wadsworth Publishing, 1990), 13.
3. Ibid., 7.
4. Rahula Walpol, *What the Buddha Taught* (New York: Grove Press, 1974).
5. Daniel Goleman, *Emotional Intelligence: Why it can matter more than IQ.* (New York, Bantam Books, 1995), 285.
6. H. Paul Jeffers (Ed.), *The Bully Pulpit: A Teddy Roosevelt Book of Quotations* (Dallas, Texas: Taylor Publishing Company, 1998).
7. Samuel Smiles, *Life and Labor; or, Characteristics of me of industry, culture and genius* (Chicago: Donohue, Henneberry & Co., 1899).
8. Wikipedia, "Puritans."
9. Conservapedia, "The Old Deluder Act."
10. Ken Curtis, "Who Were the Puritans," Christianity.com.
11. Wikipedia, "Scotch-Irish Americans."
12. Dictionary of American History, "Scotch-Irish," (The Gale Group Inc., 2003).
13. Stewart Sutherland, Baron Sutherland of Houndwood, "Scottish Enlightenment," Britanica.com.
14. BBC, "Great Thinkers of the Scottish Enlightenment."
15. Wikipedia, "Scottish Enlightenment."

16. Wikipedia, "Thomas Reid."

17. *New World Encyclopedia,* "Thomas Reid."

18. Information Philosopher, "Thomas Reid."

19. Ohio State Univeristy, "Thomas Reid – Free Will," u.osu.edu.

20. Thomas Reid. An Inquiry into the Human Mind on the Principles of Common Sense. Ed. Derek R Brookes. (Edinburgh: Edinburgh University Press, 1997).

21. Stanford Encyclopedia of Philosophy, "Thomas Reid," plato. stanford.edu.

22. Ibid.

23. Wikipedia, "Scottish Common Sense Realism."

24. The Information Philosopher, "Thomas Reid."

25. Ibid.

26. Wikipedia, "John Witherspoon."

27. USHistory.org, "Signers of the Declaration of Independence: John Witherspoon."

28. Alexander Leitch. (1978) *A Princeton Companion.* Princeton University Press: Princeton, NJ.

29. etcweb.princetown.edu, "John Witherspoon."

30. Quentin R. Skrabec, (2009). *William McGuffey: Mentor to American Industry.* (New York: Algora Publishing, 2009), 42.

31. Harvey C. Minnich, *William Holmes McGuffey and His Readers.* (New York: American Book Company: 1936), 20.

32. Skrabec, *William McGuffey: Mentor to American Industry,* 88.

33. Ibid., 44.

34. Wikipedia, "Noah Webster."

35. Skrabec, *William McGuffey: Mentor to American Industry,* 8.

36. Ibid., 9.

37. Sidney Olson and David Lanier Lewis, Young Henry Ford, (Detroit: Wayne State University Press, 1997).

38. John H. Westerhoff, *McGuffey and His Readers: Piety, Morality, and Education in Nineteenth-Century America,* Milford, MI: Mott Media, 1982), 82.

39. Henry H. Vail, *A History of the McGuffey Readers,* )(Cleveland: The Burrows Brothers Co., 1911), 2.

40. Minnich, *William Holmes McGuffey and His Readers,* 55.

41. Ibid., 80.

42. Hamlin Garland, *A Son of the Middle Border,* (St. Paul, MN: Borealis Books, 2007).

43. Ben Shapiro, "5 Times Hillary and Bernie Pandered to Blacks During the Last Debate," *Breitbart News*, March 2016.

## CHAPTER 2

1. Cheryl K. Chumley, "Charles Barkley doubles down on Ferguson: 'We as black people, we have a lot of crooks'," *The Washington Times*, December 3, 2014.
2. George Batsche and Howard Knoff. (1995). *The Use of Classroom-Based Social Skills Training to Improve Student Behavior: A Project ACHIEVE Training Manual*. University of South Florida, Tampa, FL.
3. Jerry and Nancy McMullen. (Feb 2000). *Communiqué*, Vol. 28 (5). National Association of School Psychologists: Bethesda, MD.

## CHAPTER 3

1. Jessica Bock, "State votes to strip Normandy schools of accreditation," *St. Louis Post-Dispatch*, September 18, 2012.
2. Rebecca Klein, "Michael Brown's High School Is An Example Of The Major Inequalities In Education," *Huffington Post*, August 21, 2014.
3. Elisa Crouch, "Normandy High: The most dangerous school in the area, *St. Louis Post-Dispatch*, May 05, 2013.
4. Jesse Bogan, "Troubled Normandy school district looks for answers amid empty chairs, revolving doors," *St. Louis Post-Dispatch*, May 19, 2013.
5. Christine Byers, "Normandy police chief critical of school security," *St. Louis Post-Dispatch*, January 4, 2013.
6. Joe Harris, "Student says guard school crippled him," *Courthouse News*, September 17, 2012.
7. Staff Report, "Normandy substitute teacher is accused of pulling knife on student," *St. Louis Times-Dispatch*, November 9, 2012.
8. Paul Schankman, "Normandy HS Student Dies After Punch to Chest," Fox2now, April 12, 2013.
9. Emily Wax-Thibodeaux, "At Michael Brown's former high school, students and teachers try to overcome odds," *Washington Post*, August 26, 2014.
10. Breeanna Hare, "Charles Barkley: 'Brainwashed' blacks hold up success," CNN, October 28, 2014.
11. Kareem Abdul-Jabbar and Peter Knobler, Giant Steps: The Autobiography of Kareem Abdul-Jabbar, (New York: Bantam Books, 1983), 16.

12. Jason L. Riley, *Please Stop Helping Us: How Liberals Make It Harder for Blacks to Succeed*, (New York: Encounter Books, 2014), 37.
13. Ibid. 51.
14. Ibid.
15. John Eligon, "Michael Brown Spent Last Weeks Grappling With Problems and Promise," *New York Times*, August 24, 2014.
16. Margaret Sullivan, "An Ill-Chosen Phrase, 'No Angel,' Brings a Storm of Protest," *New York Times*, August 25, 2014.
17. Jim Hoft, "Mike Brown's Rap Lyrics Surface: 'LIGHTS OUT, Gonna Knock You're a$$ Out'," *The Gateway Pundit*, August 21, 2014.
18. Doug Giles, "'GENTLE GIANT': Mike Brown's VERY Explicit Rap Songs Praising Drugs, Drinking, Ho's & Murder," *ClashDaily*, August 16, 2014.
19. Matt Hansen and Kurtis Lee, "Michael Brown's raps: Money, sex, drugs-and a vulnerable side," *Los Angeles Times*, August 21, 2014.
20. Wikipedia, "N.W.A."
21. Gil Griffin, "STRONG WORDS FROM ICE-T AND N.W.A.," *Washington Post*, June 12, 1991.
22. Alan Light, "N.W.A.: Beating Up the Charts," *Rolling Stone*, August 8, 1991.
23. Ibid.
24. Ibid.
25. CBS St. Louis/AP, "New Video Shows Brown's Stepfather Saying 'I'm Going to Start a Riot'," December 8, 2014.
26. Warner Todd Huston, "Al Sharpton Leads March in DC as NYC Protesters Chant: 'What Do We Want? Dead Cops!'" *Breitbart News*, December 13, 2014.
27. Lydia Warren, "Paramedic sparks outrage with Instagram photo showing two black men pointing guns at a white cop with the caption: 'Our real enemy,'" *Daily Mail*, December 19, 2014
28. Tricia L. Nadolny, "Uproar over Phila. paramedic's Instagram post," *Philadelphia Inquirer*, : December 20, 2014.
29. Jim Hoft, "Farrakhan Threatens to 'Tear This Godd*m Country Apart' Over Ferguson Shooting," *The Gateway Pundit*, December 1, 2014.
30. **Washington CBS Local,** "Farrakhan To African-Americans: 'Let's Die For Something,'" *December 1, 2014.*
31. Kim Barker and Al Baker, "New York Officers' Killer, Adrift and Ill, Had a Plan," *New York Times*, December 21, 2014.

32. Associated Press, "NYPD Shooting Eyewitness: People 'Clapping and Laughing' After Killings," *Breitbart News*, December 20, 2014.

33. Nedra Pickler and Jim Kuhnhenn, "Obama: No excuse for violent, destructive protest," The Associated Press, November 25, 2014.

34. Cheryl K. Chumley, "Charles Barkley doubles down on Ferguson: 'We as black people, we have a lot of crooks,'" *The Washington Times*, December 3, 2014.

## CHAPTER 4

1. *Politics*Nation with Al Sharpton, "Eyewitness to Brown Shooting Speaks Out," msnbc, August 12, 2014.

2. Trymaine Lee, "Eyewitness to Michael Brown Shooting Recounts His Friend's Death," msnbc, updated August 19, 2014.

3. All in with Chris Hayes, "Dorian Johnson: 'We Need to Stand Up for Something Better,'" msnbc, November 25, 2014.

4. Kevin Killeen, "Protestors: Police Shot 'Unarmed' Man," CBS St.Louis, May 22, 2013.

5. Joel Currier, "Fatal Shooting by St. Louis Police was Justified, Federal Investigation Says," St. Louis Post-Dispatch, June 8, 2014.

6. Leah Thorsen, "Man in Hospital Dies After Arrest by Hazelwood Police," St. Louis Post-Dispatch, July 11, 2013.

7. Jennifer S. Mann, "Wrongful Death Suit Filed Against Hazelwood Police," St. Louis Post-Dispatch, December 27, 2013.

8. Joel Currier, "Fourth-grader Shot in His St. Louis Home was 'model student,'" St. Louis Post-Dispatch, March 28, 2014.

9. Ibid.

10. Jack Healy, "Another Killing in Ferguson Leaves a Family Grappling With the Unknown, New York Times, December 1, 2014.

11. Gina Loudon, "Ferguson-Shooting Witness Wanted in 2011 Case," WorldNetDaily, August 15, 2014.

12. Sam Clancy, "Dorian Johnson Charged with Interfering with Arrest," USA Today, May 7, 2015.

13. Jeremy Kohler, "Man Stopped with Michael Brown on Aug. 9 Sues Ferguson, Police, Officer, USA Today, May 5, 2015.

14. Ben Shapiro, "Original Witnesses' 'Hands Up' Brown Stories Falling Apart," Breitbart *News*, August 19, 2014.

15. Ibid.

16. Lucy McCalmont, "Lawmakers Make 'hands up' Gesture on House Floor," *Politico*, December 2, 2014.

*WorldNetDaily*, "Preacher Stuns with 'Michael Brown is Jesus' Rant," August 28, 2014.

## CHAPTER 5

1. Tim Jones, "Barack Obama: mother not just a girl from Kansas; Stanly Ann Dunham shaped a future senator," *Chicago Tribune*, March 27, 2007.
2. Wikipedia, "1967 Detroit Riot."
3. Seligman, Martin. (1995). *The Optimistic Child*. Houghton Mifflin Company: New York, p. 40.
4. Brad Knickerbocker, "President Obama smoked pot in high school. Why is he against legalizing marijuana? *Christian Science Monitor*, May 26, 2012.
5. Punahou School, http://www.punahou.edu/about/index.aspx
6. Andrew Hamilton, "Revisiting Tom Wolfe's *Radical Chic* (1970)," *Counter-currents*, August 2014.
7. Wikipedia, "Ten-Point Program."
8. Hamilton, "Revisiting Tom Wolfe's *Radical Chic* (1970)."
9. Henry Louis Gates Jr., "How Many Slaves Landed in the US?" *The Root*, January 6 2014.
10. Henry Louis Gates Jr., "Ending the Slavery Blame-Game," *New York Times*, April 22, 2010.
11. Pam Key, "Sanders: As President I Would Formally Apologize for Slavery," *Breitbart News*, April 6, 2016.
12. Mensah M. Dean, "Phila. School District still struggling to fill teacher vacancies," *Philadelphia Inquirer*, April 12, 2016.
13. Ibid.
14. Devin Foley, "Mau-Mauing the Flak Catchers. Is this what's actually going on?" *Intellectual Takeout*, November 17, 2015.
15. Tom Wolfe, *Radical Chic & Mau-mauing the Flak Catchers* (New York: Farrar, Straus and Giroux, 2009).
16. Byron York, "What Did Obama Do as a Community Organizer?" *National Review Online*, September 8, 2008.
17. Barack Obama, *Dreams of My Father: A Story of Race and Inheritance* (New York Times Books, 1995).
18. Aaron Klein, "Obama quotes Alinsky in speech to young Israelis: Channels theme of 'Rules for Radicals' book dedicated to Lucifer," *WorldNetDaily*, March 21, 2013.
19. Serge Kovaleski, "Obama's Organizing Years, Guiding Others and Finding Himself," *New York Times*, July 7, 2008.

20. Charles C. Johnson, "The Gospel According To Wright: How much of Pastor Jeremiah Wright's race-based 'theology' does Barack Obama really share?" *American Spectator*, December 2011-January 2012.
21. Kovaleski, "Obama's Organizing Years, Guiding Others and Finding Himself."
22. York, "What Did Obama Do as a Community Organizer?"
23. Ibid.
24. Jeremy Gorner, "Chicago violence, homicides and shootings up in 2015," *Chicago Tribune*, January 2, 2016.
25. *Wikipedia*, "Crime in Chicago: Annual homicide total by year."
26. John Byrne, "Emanuel blames Chicago crime uptick on officers second-guessing themselves," *Chicago Tribune*, October 13, 2015.
27. Monica Davey, "Violence Surges in Chicago Even as Policing Debate Rages," *New York Times*, March 28, 2016.
28. Anita Padilla, "South Side woman launches 'sex strike' to end violence," *Fox 32 News*, November 18, 2015.
29. Jeremy Gorner, "Grim milestone: Chicago tops 1,000 shootings weeks earlier than recent years," *Chicago Tribune*, April 21, 2016.
30. Davey, "Violence Surges in Chicago Even as Policing Debate Rages."
31. Kelly Kennedy, "Government costs of gunshot wounds and deaths in 2010, *USA Today*, March 5, 2013.

## CHAPTER 6

1. Wikipedia, "Henry Louis Gates, Jr."
2. Michele McPhee and Sara Just, "Obama: Police Acted 'Stupidly in Gates Case," *abc NEWS*, July 22, 2009.
3. Wikipedia, "Deval Patrick."
4. Wikipedia, "Charles Ogletree."
5. Lou Jones, "Gates' Lawyer Challenges 'The Presumption Of Guilt,'" Heard on *Talk of the Nation*, June 22, 2010.
6. *Harvard Plagiarism Archive*, http://authorskeptics.blogspot.com/2004/09/professor-charles-ogletree.html
7. The Crimson Staff, "What Academia is Hiding," *The Harvard Crimson*, September 13, 2004.
8. Cambridge Police Department Incident Report #900127
9. Abby Goodnough, "Sergeant Who Arrested Professor Defends Actions," *New York Times*, July 23, 2009.
10. McPhee and Just, "Obama: Police Acted 'Stupidly' in Gates Case."
11. Ibid.

12. Goodnough, "Sergeant Who Arrested Professor Defends Actions."
13. Associated Press, "Review of Harvard Professor Arrest Finds Incident Was Avoidable," foxnews.com, June 30, 2010.
14. Don VanNatta Jr. and Abby Goodnough, "2 Cambridge Worlds Collide in Unlikely Meeting, *New York Times*, July 26, 2009.
15. TIMESVIDEO, http://www.nytimes.com/video/ us/1247463639030/cambridge-officer-breaks-his-silence.html
16. Goodnough, "Sergeant Who Arrested Professor Defends Actions."
17. Ibid.
18. Van Natta and Goodnough, "2 Cambridge Worlds Collide in Unlikely Meeting."
19. McPhee and Just, "Obama: Police Acted 'Stupidly' in Gates Case."
20. Ibid.
21. Wikipedia, "E. Denise Simmons."
22. "Henry Louis Gates '73 arrested at Harvard, charges racial profiling," *Yale Daily News*, July 20, 2009.
23. CNN Interview of Cambridge Police, July 26, 2009.
24. Beverly Ford, "Sgt. James Crowley, cop who arrested Harvard professor Henry Louis Gates Jr., denies he's racist," *New York Daily News*, July 24, 2009.
25. Van Natta and Goodnough, "2 Cambridge Worlds Collide in Unlikely Meeting."
26. Goodnough, "Sergeant Who Arrested Professor Defends Actions."
27. Peter Baker and Helene Cooper, "Obama Shifts Tone on Gates After Mulling Debate," *New York Times*, July 25, 2009.
28. Ibid.
29. Krissah Thompson, "Arrest of Harvard's Henry Louis Gates Jr. was avoidable, report says," *Washington Post*, June 30, 2010.
30. Helene Cooper and Abby Goodnough, "Over Beers, No Apologies, but Plans to Have Lunch," *New York Times*, July 30, 2009.
31. Ibid.
32. Elizabeth Gates, "What I Saw at the Beer Summit," *The Daily Beast*, July 31, 2009.
33. John Sexton, "Van Jones: Obama 'Forced' to Sit with 'Racist' Cop at Beer Summit," *Breitbart News*, April 17, 2012.
34. Glenn Beck, "We Love You Too, Van Jones," *Fox News*, March 1, 2010.
35. WorldNetDaily, "Years after resignation, commentary cites revelations about 'Green Jobs Czar,'" October 28, 2011.

36. Wikipedia, Van Jones.

## CHAPTER 7
1. "Obama's full remarks at Howard University commencement ceremony," *Politico Magazine*, May 7, 2016.
2. Warner Todd Huston, "Obama: Crime Created by 'System,' Successful People 'Just Lucky,' 'Wasn't Nothin' You Did'." *Breitbart News*, May 10, 2016.
3. Jason L. Riley, *Please Stop Helping Us: How Liberals Make It Harder for Blacks to Succeed*, (New York: Encounter Books, 2014),

## AFTERWORD
1. James Webb, "Heroes of the Vietnam Generation." American Enterprise Institute, July/August 2000.
2. Alan Waugh, "The Duc Duc Resettlement Village Massacre." http://home.earthlink.net/~ducducvietnamfriends/an_unknown_massacre_in_vietnam/id8.html.
3. Colin Flaherty, White Girl Bleed A Lot, Washington, D.C.: WND Books, Inc, 2013), p. 5.
4. Craig Bannister, "Obama: Police Can 'Make the Job of Being a Cop a Lot Safer' by Admitting Their Failures," July 11, 2016, http://www.mrctv.org/blog/obama-police-can-make-job-being-cop-lot-safer-admitting-their-failures.
5. Victor Morton, "Baton Rouge officer's Facebook post goes viral after ambush death," The Washington Times, July 17, 2016.
6. Chicago tribune staff, "After another violent weekend, Chicago police say 'everyone' needs to step up and help," Chicago Tribune, July 18, 2016.

www.ingramcontent.com/pod-product-compliance
Lightning Source LLC
Chambersburg PA
CBHW020002290326
41935CB00007B/272